Kundalini

KUNDALINI

THE SACRED FIRE
OF ALL RELIGIONS

SAMAEL AUN WEOR

GLORIAN

Kundalini
A Glorian Book / 2023

Originally published in Spanish as "Los Misterios del Fuego" (1955).

This Edition © 2023 Glorian Publishing

ISBN 978-1-943358-20-5

Glorian Publishing is a non-profit organization. All proceeds further the
distribution of these books. For more information, visit glorian.org

Contents

Illustrations

Editor's Notes

As a response to *Kundalini Yoga* by his friend Swami Sivananda (1887–1963), Samael Aun Weor published *Mysteries of the Fire* in 1955. It was his fourteenth book in five years, and continued the themes of his most recent writings, notably *Treatise of Sexual Alchemy* (1954), a highly detailed and challenging book, especially for any reader not already well-versed in alchemical terms and symbolism. Samael Aun Weor did not spoon-feed the reader, or tiptoe into the waters of esotericism; instead, he plunged the reader right into the deepest waters, and kept going... He did the same with *Mysteries of the Fire*, except one needed to know the Sanskrit terms and structures of Yoga. The first page is packed with Sanskrit words; we can only imagine how the average reader in 1955 would have understood it, as Yoga was only just starting to enter the public eye.

Years ago, we published the first English edition of this book as it had been written, save for the title: in the internet age, we felt that the title *Kundalini Yoga* would attract more readers than *Mysteries of the Fire* would. Yet the content was simply too difficult for readers. That first page was really tough.

In his later writings, Samael Aun Weor developed a much more approachable style; he was still equal parts ferocious and insightful, but also personable, accessible, and deeply compassionate. He took more time to explain things to his readers, and guide them on towards deeper subjects. So, we have brought that gentler pace into this edition. We have added a Prologue of a few of his lectures, more than one hundred footnotes, and an extensive glossary. With all of this, you will be better prepared for the journey through *The Mysteries of the Fire*. In fact, by understanding it better, the journey will be even more powerful than it would have been otherwise.

We wish you Godspeed.

Prologue

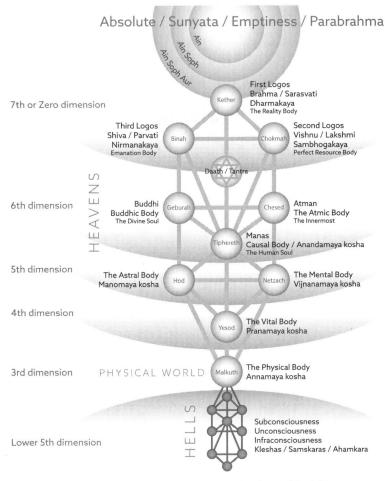

Absolute / Sunyata / Emptiness / Parabrahma

Ain
Ain Soph
Ain Soph Aur

7th or Zero dimension

Kether — First Logos
Brahma / Sarasvati
Dharmakaya
The Reality Body

Third Logos
Shiva / Parvati
Nirmanakaya
Emanation Body — Binah

Chokmah — Second Logos
Vishnu / Lakshmi
Sambhogakaya
Perfect Resource Body

Daath / Tantra

HEAVENS

6th dimension

Buddhi
Buddhic Body
The Divine Soul — Geburah

Chesed — Atman
The Atmic Body
The Innermost

Manas
Tiphereth — Causal Body / Anandamaya kosha
The Human Soul

5th dimension

The Astral Body
Manomaya kosha — Hod

Netzach — The Mental Body
Vijnanamaya kosha

4th dimension

Yesod — The Vital Body
Pranamaya kosha

3rd dimension

PHYSICAL WORLD — Malkuth — The Physical Body
Annamaya kosha

HELLS

Lower 5th dimension

Subconsciousness
Unconsciousness
Infraconsciousness
Kleshas / Samskaras / Ahamkara

Hindu Philosophy on the Tree of Life (Kabbalah)

The Power to Create and Destroy
A Lecture Given by Samael Aun Weor

What exactly is the object of these studies? For what purpose? What is our objective? What do we want? This is something that all of us must reflect deeply on.

First of all, I want you to know that behind this Sun that illuminates us and gives us life is the sacred solar Absolute.[1] Each one of us has in the sacred Absolute the very root of our Being.

We have been told a lot about the Ain Soph[2] Paranishpanna;[3] this Ain Soph is the inner star that has always smiled on us. A very wise author said, "I raise my eyes to the stars from which help will come to me, but I always follow (the Ain Soph) the star that guides me inside..."

That star is the Ain Soph Paranishpanna.

Undoubtedly, my dear brothers and sisters, from the Ain Soph emanates the incessant eternal breath, profoundly unknowable to itself: the active omnipresent, omnipenetrating, omniscient Okidanokh.[4]

Undoubtedly, from that active Okidanokh, from that tremendous ray that unites us to the Ain Soph Paranishpanna (located as we already said in the sacred solar Absolute), the three primary forces *become*. We call the first Holy Affirming, the second Holy Denying, and the third Holy Reconciling. In the Hindustani terms, the first could be called Brahma, the second, Vishnu, and the third, Shiva. They are the three forces: positive, negative, and neutral. Each of us, in ourselves,

---

1 Fundamental reality. See glossary.
2 Hebrew אֵין סוֹף "infinite, no end, limitless"
3 Sanskrit परिनिष्पन्न, "real, perfect, existing. Absolute truth, Absolute happiness." This is essentially Sat-Chit-Ananda "Existence-Knowledge-Bliss."
4 A term utilized by Gurdjieff to describe the light or ray of creation, the primary emanation of the Ain Soph Aur, the Solar Absolute. Okidanokh is the fundamental cause of all cosmic phenomena; it is the Christic substance capable of penetrating all cosmic formations. Kabbalistically, it is the life source of the sacred Triamazikamno / Trimurti / Trinity.

particularly, have that ray that unites us to the great reality. Each of us, in ourselves, have these three forces. In short, each one of us is connected to the sacred solar Absolute.

Thus, thinking in a macrocosmic manner, no longer only from the point of view of the microcosmic human, we will see how the holy omnipenetrating, omniscient Okidanokh remains involved in the worlds, but not imprisoned in the worlds.

During manifestation, the Holy Okidanokh emanates from itself the three forces for creation. Without these three forces (positive, negative, neutral), creation would be impossible.

If we carefully observe the creatures of nature, we see that the cephalopod animals—that is, with only one brain—such as snails, insects that last only a summer afternoon, mollusks, etc., express only one force. In bicephalous or higher order animals such as birds, quadrupeds, etc., two forces are manifested. Only in the intellectual animal[5] mistakenly called human, the three forces are expressed.[6] That is why only the intellectual animal could crystallize within itself the three primary forces of nature. And that, precisely that, my dear brothers and sisters, is what the sacred solar Absolute wants.

It is our duty to fight to achieve, in ourselves, the crystallization of these three primary forces of nature. When someone manages to crystallize the three primary forces in themselves, they undoubtedly reach the Logoic state, reach the goal, and earn the right to return to the sacred Absolute Sun.

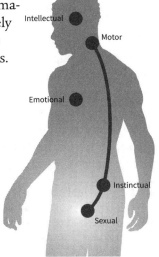

Our Three Brains

---

5   An animal with intellect. See glossary.
6   We have three brains: the intellectual brain, the emotional brain, and the motor-instinctual-sexual brain. They process, respectively: thoughts, emotions, and impulses.

That is precisely what the sacred solar Absolute wants in the psychophysiological, in the psychosomatic, etc., to perform within us, which is, the crystallization of the three primary forces of nature.

Only in this way can we become what is called the Celestial Adam, the Adam Kadmon[7] that the Kabbalists speak about.

Let us reflect, we are called, then, to crystallize these three forces of nature within ourselves, here and now.

Who is the Master Kuthumi? He is a man who crystallized the three primary forces within himself. Who is Morya? He is a man who crystallized those three forces within himself. Who is Jesus of Nazareth? He is a man who managed to crystallize those three forces in himself. Who is Sanat Kumara? He is someone who managed to crystallize, in himself, the three primary forces of nature and the cosmos.

Listen my dear brothers and sisters, the incarnation of the three primary forces is not a simple enterprise. If we fill a glass with water, it can be lost when the glass overturns or breaks; another thing is to crystallize that water inside the glass so it remains fixed, firm. The same happens, my dear brothers and sisters, with the Logos:[8] if we only incarnated it, it would remain just an inhabitant, something like water in a glass, it can escape; it would no longer be there inside our body, but visiting. Thus, crystallizing it is different, and that is precisely what we need.

But let's go to the bottom of this, my dear brothers and sisters: we want to know our purpose. It is obvious that each one of us can become a Logos, it is obvious that each one of us can achieve the crystallization of the three primary forces, in ourselves, here and now. The important thing is to know how, the procedure, the method, the system that does not fail,

---

7   The first manifestation of the abstract space; the archetypal human; humanity; the heavenly human, not fallen into sin.

8   Greek λόγος, from λέγω lego "I say," means Verb or Word. The unifying principle. The Logos is the manifested deity of every nation and people; the outward expression or the effect of the cause which is ever concealed. (Speech is the "logos" of thought). The Logos has three aspects, known universally as the Trinity, Trikaya, or Trimurti. These are related to the three primary forces behind all forms of creation.

that is exact, that is precise; and luckily, that is what you are
going to learn here.

Kundalini

First of all, if we really want to achieve the crystallization
of the three primary forces within ourselves here and now, we
have to start by awakening the Kundalini,[9] the igneous serpent of our magical powers.

> *"Kundalini, the serpent power or mystic fire, is the
> primordial energy or Sakti that lies dormant or
> sleeping in the Muladhara Chakra, the centre of the
> body. It is called the serpentine or annular power on
> account of serpentine form. It is an electric fiery occult
> power, the great pristine force which underlies all
> organic and inorganic matter. Kundalini is the cosmic
> power in individual bodies. It is not a material force
> like electricity, magnetism, centripetal or centrifugal
> force. It is a spiritual potential Sakti or cosmic power.
> In reality it has no form. [...] O Divine Mother
> Kundalini, the Divine Cosmic Energy that is hidden in
> men! Thou art Kali, Durga, Adisakti, Rajarajeswari,
> Tripurasundari, Maha-Lakshmi, Maha-Sarasvati!
> Thou hast put on all these names and forms. Thou
> hast manifested as Prana, electricity, force, magnetism,
> cohesion, gravitation in this universe. This whole
> universe rests in Thy bosom. Crores of salutations unto
> thee. O Mother of this world! Lead me on to open the
> Sushumna Nadi and take Thee along the Chakras to
> Sahasrara Chakra and to merge myself in Thee and
> Thy consort, Lord Siva. Kundalini Yoga is that Yoga
> which treats of Kundalini Sakti, the six centres of
> spiritual energy (Shat Chakras), the arousing of the
> sleeping Kundalini Sakti and its union with Lord Siva
> in Sahasrara Chakra, at the crown of the head. This is
> an exact science."* —Swami Sivananda, Kundalini Yoga

---

9   Sanskrit कुण्डलिनी, from kundala, "coiled." The power of the Divine Moth-
     er that awakens in those who earn it. Also called Pentecost (Christiani-
     ty), Shekinah (Judaism), Quetzalcoatl (Aztec), etc.

Shiva and Shakti (Parvati)
Hindu symbol of the Third
Logos. Shiva represents the
impelling force of creation
and destruction, while Shakti
is the power that fulfills it.
Shiva wills it, Shakti makes it
happen. Shakti (power) is the
Divine Mother Kundalini.

The Kundalini-shakti[10] is also prana,[11] life. It is coiled three and a half times inside the Muladhara chakra;[12] that magnetic center is located exactly in the coccygeal bone.[13] In Christian esotericism it is known as the "church of Ephesus."[14]

There are many procedures with which people want to awaken the Kundalini. I once saw in a film something very curious that happens in the lands of Hindustan (something

---

10 Sanskrit शक्ति "force, power, energy" from the root sakt, "to be able, to do." Shakti is symbolized as a goddess, the wife of Shiva, the Third Logos, the sephirah Binah. A personification of primal energy. Symbolized by a yoni, a female sexual organ.

11 Sanskrit प्राण life-principle; the breath of life; energy.

12 Sanskrit चक्र "wheel, circle." In Asian traditions, the word chakra refers to any wheel or circle, and is often used to describe circular weapons used by the gods. Most people today associate the word with subtle centers of energetic transformation that are within our bodies. There are hundreds of chakras in our multi-dimensional physiology, but seven primary ones related to the awakening of consciousness.

13 At the base of the spine.

14 In the Revelation or Apocalypse of St. John.

barbaric, by the way): a yogi appeared there with that coccygeal bone exposed, uncovered; they had opened that part
with a knife, that is, they had removed the skin that covers
the bone, and even the meat itself had been opened. The procedure was barbaric. Another yogi was intensively rubbing
the victim's coccyx with a cloth, with of course the objective
of awakening the Kundalini. That is a barbaric system, obviously; the way he moved that rag was very similar to the procedure used by shoe polishers to clean shoes, and it inflicted
pain on that yogi... Of course, this is due to ignorance. This is
not how the igneous serpent of our magical powers awakens.
She never awakens through procedures like this.

Others try to awaken Devi[15] Kundalini through pranayama[16]—inhaling through the right nostril, holding it, exhaling
through the left and vice versa; controlling the breath with
the index finger and thumb. I do not deny the value of pranayama—it is great for vitalizing the physical body, but it does
not serve to awaken Devi Kundalini, the igneous serpent of
our magical powers. Some sparks might jump from the coccyx, which circulate through the nadis or organic channels
and bring moments of illumination, then the yogi believes
that he has awakened the Kundalini, but no, the Kundalini
remains, it is still coiled inside the Muladhara chakra.

Some suppose that some holy man can stretch his hand
over the disciple to awaken the igneous snake, but that concept is also wrong.

The magical serpent only awakens, my dear brothers and
sisters, with a single procedure: the Sahaja Maithuna.[17] I have
taught it in all my works. I have repeated it in all classes ad
nauseam. Due to this, some calls us "sex freaks" because peo-

---

15 Sanskrit देवी "goddess, queen."
16 Sanskrit प्राणायाम for "restraint (ayama) of energy, life force (prana)." A
    type of breathing exercise which transforms the life force (sexual energy)
    of the practitioner.
17 Sanskrit सहज sahaja "original, natural," मैथुन maithuna "marriage, sacra-
    mental intercourse, a pair or one of each sex." A reference to superior
    sexuality in which the orgasm is abandoned and lust is replaced by love.
    Also called alchemy, tantra, Oordhvareta Yoga, Christian Syneisaktism.

ple seeks evasions, justifications for weaknesses, loopholes, self-deception, etc.

Once, while in the state of samadhi or satori, I asked Devi Kundalini, "Is it possible that there in the physical world there is someone who can attain self-realization without the need for sexual magic?"[18]

The answer was terrible, "Impossible, my son, that is not possible!"

Our True Condition

I was left reflecting; when we think of so many sincerely mistaken people that abound in the world, who believe that through celibacy they can reach the intimate self-realization of their Being, one cannot help but feel true compassion for humanity. Those who think this way, those who defend celibacy, deep down, "not only ignore, but also ignore that they ignore"; "not only do they not know, but also, they do not know that they do not know." If they had their spatial sense completely awake, they could verify for themselves, directly, the harsh reality of the "intellectual animal"; then they would fully realize that they do not really possess those supersensible bodies that the pseudo-esotericists and pseudo-occultists speak about.

When someone who has really developed the chakras carefully studies people, one can fully realize that all people have only one body: the physical body, and nothing else.

The seat of life, the Linga Sarira[19] of the Hindustani, the Mumia of Paracelsus, what of it? This is really nothing more than the four-dimensional section of the same physical body.

And beyond that physical body with its vital seat, what is it, really, that people have? The ego. They do have something else: the ego, the I, the myself, the self-willed.

This ego can be confused with the astral body, as many pseudo-esotericists and pseudo-occultists have already con-

---

18 Magic comes from magi, "priest." See glossary.
19 The vital body, also called chi, jing, aura, etc.

fused it; not only did they confuse it in the past, but they still keep confusing it.

The ego is a sum of negative values; a bunch of passions, hatred, jealousy, mistrust, fornication, etc. This ego is not the astral body.

Getting to see this reality is necessary, but it is only possible through the awakening of the chakras. Getting to see this crude reality of the intellectual animal is very important. Only one who awakens the consciousness can verify this. The unconscious, the asleep, could never verify this truth.

The various pseudo-esoteric and pseudo-occult schools of thought tell us that "the humanoid has a mental body." I accept this for a human; but I could not accept it for the intellectual animal mistakenly called human.

I repeat, the three-brained biped, or the rational homunculus to be clearer, does not have a mental body, does not have a mind; it has "minds," which is different. Let me explain: if the ego is a sum of psychic aggregates, or pernicious entities that personify our errors, it is obvious that each of them has a mind of its own.

Speaking in different terms, I will say: the ego is a sum of "I's." There is not one "I," but many "I's" within each individual. This may be a little understood by some, and yet we must all understand it.

The "I" of anger, the "I" of hatred, the "I" of fornication, the "I" of envy, the "I" of violence, etc. are different "I's." The cannot be seen with the naked eye, but with the spatial sense they are. Whoever has the spatial sense will be able to verify what I am saying.

That set of "I's" is very varied and constitutes the ego.

Each one of those "I's" has its own mind, it is true...

When we are full of hate, we see everything dark, black. When we are full of envy, we see everything green, we dislike the triumphs of others, etc.

When we have plans in our mind, we feel that we are "geniuses."

Each I that controls the capital centers of the organic machine feels like the master, the lord, the only one, the boss.

The one who today swears eternal love to someone is displaced tomorrow by another "I" that has nothing to do with that oath.

The "I" that today is enthusiastic about these studies, that attends this center, is displaced tomorrow by another "I" that has nothing to do with these studies, and then we see how the subject leaves, to never return.

We are machines controlled by many perverse entities. We are not individuals. We have not yet individualized ourselves. We are in a sorry state, but we believe we are "gods." We must reflect on this deeply.

Likewise, if today the mind thinks one thing, tomorrow it is displaced by a mind that thinks something else.

The "intellectual animal" does not have a mental body.

Finding ourselves, then, in these conditions, we must reflect...

We are told that "we have a causal body" (so the pseudo-esotericists say, so the pseudo-occultists emphasize). But the causal body is the body of conscious will. The one who has conscious will is never a victim of circumstances; that one can determine them, yes, at will, but not be a victim of them. One who is a victim of circumstances does not have a body of conscious will, does not possess it, because if one possessed it, one would not be a victim of circumstances.

However, the pseudo-occultists believe that the humanoid has that body of the conscious will while the facts show the opposite. Facts are facts, and before the facts we have to surrender.

Thus, the only thing we have inside is the "beast," the animal ego.

There is something more decent that we have, yes. The essence[20] is the most elevated thing that we have inside. But this essence is bottled up within that collection of quarrelsome and loud-mouthed "I's." Thus, the essence is processed according to its conditioning.

That is the state we find ourselves in, my dear brothers and sisters. The only panacea that the enlightened ignorants of pseudo-occultism and cheap pseudo-esotericism give us is "celibacy." Do you really believe that such absurd celibacy could make us gods? There we have entire communities (I don't want to name any), of religious celibates: which of them has attained self-realization?

The Law of Creation

In a man, or in the intellectual animal mistakenly called human, although the three forces can manifest themselves, really only one activates in all its power and in all its fullness, the first: the holy affirmation (+). In the intellectual animal called woman, the second force is active, the holy negation (-). If you want to make a creation, obviously, you need to activate the three forces; that is the mystery of creation. When the holy affirming and the holy denying are reconciled by the third force (=), when they are united by a third force, when these three merge, a creation results: a child, or a monster, or whatever, but something has been created.

If you want to create the astral body (about which Philip Theophrastus Bombastus von Hohenheim spoke), the eidolon, the sidereal vehicle, obviously, we have to use the three

---

20 From the Chinese 體 ti, which literally means "substance, body" and is often translated as "essence," to indicate that which is always there throughout transformations. In gnosis, the term essence refers to our consciousness, which remains fundamentally the same, in spite of the many transformations it suffers, especially life, death, and being trapped in psychological defects. A common example given in Buddhism is a glass of water: even if filled with dirt and impurities, the water is still there. However, one would not want to drink it that way. Just so with the Essence (the consciousness): our Essence is trapped in impurities; to use it properly, it must be cleaned first.

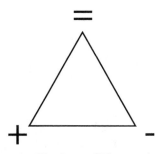

The Law of Three
The trinity of all religions represents the law of three, the
law of creation. For instance, the only way to create a child
is by a man (+) and a woman (-) united sexually (=).

primary forces of nature; thenceforth, man and woman united in the forge of the cyclops, can create the astral body.

The important thing is, as we already know, not to extract
the sacred sperm[21] [sexual power, whether in men or women]
from the organism, rather, transmute it and convert it into
energy. When it is wisely transmuted, the result is the crystallization of the astral body within our own organism.

Much later we will have to create the body of the mind. It
is through love, through sexual union of man and woman
that we can create that wonderful instrument; and finally, the
body of conscious will.

We have already clearly talked about what sexual hydrogen
Si-12 is. We have said that by not spending the sperm, by not
extracting it from the organism, the hydrogen contained there
comes to crystallize in the figure of the astral body; we have
also said that such hydrogen, not being eliminated, transforms into the mental, and finally, into the causal.

We need sexual union to completely create the superior
existential bodies of the Being. This is precisely what the
enlightened ignorants do not know; only the one who has
created the superior existential bodies can truly incarnate
the human soul within oneself, and become a human with a

---

21 Greek σπέρμα (spérma) literally means "that which is sown," and is used
     for "the seed of plants, also of animals." Since to grow human beings
     the seeds of both sexes are required, the word sperm or semen actually
     means the sexual seed of both males and females.

Jesus teaching Nicodemus about the second
birth: the creation of the soul.

"But as many as received him, to them gave he power to become the
children of God, even to them that have faith on his name: which were
born, not of blood [lineage], nor of the will of the flesh [orgasm], nor of
the will of man [statutes], but of God." –Christian Bible, John 1:12-13

"There was a man of the Pharisees, named Nicodemus, a ruler of the
Jews: The same came to Jesus by night, and said unto him, Rabbi, we
know that thou art a teacher come from God: for no man can do these
miracles that thou doest, except God be with him. Jesus answered and
said unto him, Verily, verily, I say unto thee, Except a man be born
again, he cannot see the kingdom of God. Nicodemus saith unto him,
How can a man be born when he is old? can he enter the second time
into his mother's womb, and be born? Jesus answered, Verily, verily, I
say unto thee, Except a man be born of water [sex] and of the [Holy]
Spirit, he cannot enter into the kingdom of God. That which is born of
the flesh [through common sex] is flesh; and that which is born of the
Spirit [through immaculate sexuality, as required in Leviticus 15] is spirit.
Marvel not that I said unto thee, Ye must be born again [for everything
that exists is born of sex, so must the soul be. Remember Luke 21:19:
"With patience shall ye possess thy souls."]" —Christian Bible, John 3

soul, a true human. And only authentic humans can aspire to self-realization; before that, before such longing, we must become humans.

Thus, brothers and sisters, the Kundalini only awakens through sexual contact, and the superior existential bodies of the Being can only be created through the Sahaja Maithuna, in the forge of the Cyclops.

Intellectual animals are not humans, but they think that they are. They have within themselves the seed that, if developed, transforms them into humans. It is necessary to make a revolution of the seed itself, in order to become humans.

Celibacy is, therefore, the opposite, because through celibacy one cannot create the superior existential bodies of the Being. A single force, the masculine, could not create the superior existential bodies of the Being. A single force, the feminine, could not create such supersensible vehicles. The union of the masculine force and the feminine force is needed, through the conciliation of the third force. The three forces can indeed originate new creations; that is what many enlightened ignorants do not understand.

Create the Soul, Destroy the Impurities

The Sahaja Maithuna has various transcendent and transcendental aspects. In the Sahaja Maithuna there is "solve et coagula," that is, "dissolve and coagulate": dissolve the ego, the I, the myself, and coagulate the sexual hydrogen Si-12 in the form of the superior existential bodies of the Being. That is the way to become authentic, legitimate, and true humans.

Once converted into humans (in the fullest sense of the word), one can aspire to the supreme Christification. Through the Sahaja Maithuna we create the superior existential bodies of the Being, and also using the lance of Longinus or the lance of Achilles, in those instants, we can disintegrate the "I," the myself, the ego.

Some human beings want to run away, go to the mountains, become vegetarians, etc., and they think that this way they can be self-realized. Truly, I tell you: we need to live in

Durga

The Divine Mother uses the Holy Lance to slay the
demon that symbolizes our defects (pride, envy, anger,
lust, etc). She rides a lion (the law of karma), who
stands atop a slain buffalo (our animal desires).

society, in the world, because it is in coexistence that we discover ourselves; the hidden defects that we carry surface, and if we are alert and vigilant then we see them.

A discovered defect must be submitted to analysis and meditation, and once comprehended, then we proceed by eliminating it.

So, there is a need to comprehend and eliminate. We could comprehend that we have the defect of envy, yet continue with it. It is necessary to eliminate it, and it is only possible to eliminate it in the forge of the Cyclops, that is, in the maithuna. Then we ask the mother Kundalini to eliminate this or that error, and she will do so, and we will be free from that error. But previously, it is essential to have fully comprehended it in each of the 49 levels of the subconsciousness.

In coexistence, we prepare the way for the crystallization of the second force (-).

In coexistence we prepare the way by crystallizing the third force, that of the Holy Spirit, that of the holy conciliation (=); we crystallize it by working in the forge of the cyclops.

In coexistence we discover our errors. An error discovered and eliminated is replaced by a virtue, by a quality. Then, in coexistence, in relations with humanity, we accumulate within each of us the essential values for the crystallization of the second force (-). And if we learn to obey the Father "in heaven as well as on earth," we undoubtedly prepare the way for the crystallization of the first force (+).

Therefore, coexistence is essential for the crystallization of the three primary forces.

However, those who have already dissolved the ego,[22] who have already created the superior existential bodies of the Being, who no longer possess subhuman subjective elements within their interior system or within their intimate microcosm, can afford to seek solitude, because it is in solitude that the powers of the adept are fortified. However, seeking solitude when we have not yet dissolved the ego is absurd.

Something about Gautama, Shakyamuni Buddha, comes to my mind right now. Gautama the Buddha spoke out against

22 Masters who have died and resurrected.

The Tempting Serpent of Eden Uses Lust

the abominable Kundabuffer organ; you already know that this organ was developed in archaic humanity.[23] I am referring to a certain tenebrous Luciferian fire that rushes from the coccyx downwards towards the atomic infernos of a person.

> *"In the human being, the Cosmic Mother assumes the form of the serpent. There are two serpents, the tempting serpent of Eden, which is the Goddess Kali, the abominable Kundabuffer organ; and there is the bronze serpent that healed the Israelites in the wilderness, the Kundalini serpent. These are the two feminine principles of the universe, the Virgin and the Harlot, the Divine Mother or White Moon and Astaroth, Kali, or Black Moon, which refers to its tenebrous aspect...*

> *"In synthesis, there are two great fires: the sacred fire of Kundalini which ascends through the dorsal spine, and the Kundabuffer which descends, precipitating downwards towards the infernos.*

> *"Kundalini is the serpent of bronze which healed the Israelites in the wilderness, the serpent which Moses rose upon the staff. The Kundabuffer fire is the tempting serpent of Eden, which descends downwards towards the atomic infernos of the human being. In Egyptian wisdom, this tempting serpent receives the name of Apep. In the rituals of ancient Egypt, Apep was portrayed in wax and with its head aiming downwards. Thus, they exorcised it and conjured it.*

> *"The initiate must fight against this tempting serpent of sexual passion, against this horrible Apep. The initiate must fight to the death.*

> *"This negative fire of Apep is the negative aspect of Prakriti, in other words Kali. Kali assumes the aspect of a horrible viper which is writhing in the mud (see the life of Krishna). If we want to defeat this viper in the cosmos, we must first defeat it within ourselves...*

---

23 Read *The Elimination of Satan's Tail* by Samael Aun Weor.

Vajrasattva

Derived from vajra "phallus, thunderbolt, pillar, hard, cross, impenetrable, mighty, name of Durga" and sattva, "essence, energy, wisdom, spirit, first" which altogether mean, "essence of the sexual, creative power." A symbol of Tibetan Buddhist Tantra.

"Meditate on the supreme and unchanging [emptiness/bliss]. With vajra [male sexual organ] placed inside lotus [female sexual organ], brings the winds [vital forces] into the drops [bodhichitta/sexual power], the drops into the chakras; the movement of drops halted at the vajra [male sexual organ], always rigid, the yogi continually raises fluid [never releasing it]. With the yoga of mahamudra [great seal], the descent to the vajra, and by its blessing, the instances of supreme unchanging [emptiness/bliss], completed at 21,600, will bring the great enlightenment, the attainment of Vajrasattva [diamond soul]." —Ornament of Stainless Light, an Exposition of Kalachakra Tantra, by Khedrug Norsang Gyatso

"We most not forget that we have a very terrible legion of devils, which is "Kali," the abominable Kundabuffer organ, the frightful "Apopi" serpent. People are victims of Kali, the tempting serpent of which the Hindus speak." —Samael Aun Weor, Tarot and Kabbalah

In the past, the intellectual animal had the abominable Kundabuffer organ excessively developed. It is clear that when the gods eliminated that organ, all of humanity was left with the results of that organ. The bad consequences of the abominable Kundabuffer organ are, undoubtedly, all those psychic aggregates that constitute the ego, the myself, the "I." Gautama the Buddha, comprehending that, pronounced himself against the abominable Kundabuffer organ. His entire doctrine is against that organ of abominations, against that tail of Satan that the tenebrous ones wear.

His doctrine was wonderful: in public he taught the dissolution of the ego, and in secret he taught sexual magic, and admonished his disciples, inviting them to sacrifice for humanity.

After Gautama Shakyamuni Buddha disincarnated,[24] a group of sectarians decided to create monasteries in Eastern Tibet. They emigrated from India, and settled in the Himalayas. Each of the applicants emigrated with his wife, he took his wife with him. That conglomerate was a people of true mystics, anchorites...

When the buildings were established for the groups of hermits who aspired to the dissolution of the ego and who interpreted the doctrine of Gautama in a somewhat negative way, the protests of the women came: they were horrified when they saw the kind of hermitages those anchorites were going to lock themselves within; half of the buildings had cells, the other half was for general services... Seeing those strange cells where the hermits were going to lock themselves up caused fear: they were small rooms, where there was barely a small hole through which the temple servants put food for the penitent, that is, those monks practically became prisoners...

---

24 He predicted that within five hundred years of his death, his teachings would be so degenerated as to be unrecognizable.

Something very similar to what happened in that time of the colonization, where so many became cloistered, kept between four walls, without ever being able to get out of there again. Undoubtedly many women protested, and there was a division between groups. Some, obeying their wives, left. Others, faithful to their purpose, settled a little further afield, migrated a little further, and established their monasteries. This resulted in two kinds of monasteries being established: ones that could be called "orthodox" and others a little more liberal.

The orthodox became unbearable. Each monk entered a cloister in one of those hermitages; he was a man sentenced to death. Through a hole they put food, consisting of bread and water, nothing more, until he died.

Whoever retrieved the food, who served the hermits, naturally aspired to take their place in some cell, in one of those corners. When a hermit died, he was removed from there, he was buried or his body was cremated, and whoever had brought his food happily went in to replace him. That was something abominable. The goal was to dissolve the ego, but how!

We, my dear brothers and sisters, would never accept such a monastic life. It is terrible, absurd! That is not the way.

The most serious thing is that those cloistered men abandoned their wives. They aspired to die within themselves in order to immerse themselves in nirvana; it is obvious that this is a terrible interpretation of the doctrine of Gautama, the Buddha.

Why run away from women? Why look at her as something sinful, if it is through her that self-realization can be achieved?[25]

---

25 "With an altruistic desire to aid all sentient beings,
Serving women through love, the yogin gains power.
Power is bestowed instantaneously —
For that reason the yogin should serve women.
Woman is heaven and woman is truth,
Woman is the highest ascetic path,
The Buddha is woman and women are the community,
And woman is perfect wisdom." — Candamaharosana tantra

Why run away from society? That is only to run away from oneself. By running away from society, we are only running away from ourselves, and that is absurd. Because in relation to humanity, in contact with the world, is how we come to discover the defects that we carry inside, and in relation to the opposite sex is how we can create the superior existential bodies of the Being: so why run away?

Many hermit monks in the Middle Ages followed similar customs.

We are now in the twentieth century, beginning the era of the Aquarius. Asceticism has not been renounced, no; the ascetic of this new age is different: if the past ascetic fled from sex, the Aquarius ascetics embrace sex, because they know that in sex is the marvelous power that can radically transform us. Our ascetics, then, do not avoid sex, they look towards sex.

Single life is only for those who have already achieved the elimination of the ego and the crystallization at least of the third force. But those who do not possess superior existential bodies of the Being, those who have not finished with the myself, with the "I," what are they looking for in solitude? Why do they want the path of celibacy? Why do they yearn to live an absurd life, like that of the misguided Himalayan monks that I mentioned?

We are going towards a revolution of the consciousness, to make a radical transformation. Within each of us there are extraordinary powers that are dormant, latent; we need to wake them up, put them into activity. It is only possible to achieve that when we enliven the fire and dissolve the ego. You have to enliven the flame of the spirit with the force of love. Unfortunately, people do not understand what we are saying because they are asleep. We advocate for the awakening of the consciousness, only in this way is it possible to comprehend.

My dear brothers and sisters, we must be practical. It is only possible to prove what I am saying by waking up.

Astral Projection

Those who have already begun the work of awakening must urgently learn how to consciously go out in the astral body. If they do not have the astral body, learn to go out in the essence.

We say "astral body" in a symbolic or allegorical way, or conventionally, because people don't have it.

There are moments in life when one can escape from the physical body at will, to see, hear, touch and feel the great realities that I am talking about. One of those moments, my dear brothers and sisters, is the one's between wakefulness and sleep. In those moments in which we are sleepy (not asleep, I clarify: sleepy) we can escape from the physical body at will. If in those moments we are alert and vigilant as a sentinel in times of war, we can achieve it. The important thing is to monitor the dream, become spies of our own dream, and then, when the first dreams begin, feeling ourselves to be spirit, fluid, something intangible, get out of bed.

When I speak like this, it must be translated into deeds. It is not about thinking that you are going to get up, or thinking that you are thinking, etc. What matters is doing it. Doing so—actually getting up—will produce the projection of the personality. At such moments, standing... we look back to see what is left there on the bed, we will see, with astonishment, that our physical body has remained.

And so, outside the body, we can move away from the bedroom, go out into the street, float in the atmosphere, search, inquire, investigate, discover the mysteries of life and death.

When we sleep, we all escape from the physical body...

At the precise moment of awakening, in such moments, if we close our eyes, we must imagine ourselves at the last point in which we were dreaming. Suppose we were dreaming in the Zócalo [public plaza] of Mexico and then woke up. What are we going to do?

1. Do not move on the bed.

2. Vividly imagine the Zócalo, and with the imagination try to follow the dream where we went. We close our eyes to fall asleep, intentionally reliving the dream with our imagination

as it was going, and following it as it was going. Close our eyes and try to follow the dream intensively, as it was going. If we were talking to someone, continue the conversation with that someone. Through a flashback, in time, we do fall asleep again. The result will be that the projection will take place, we will see them again in that dream, but in a different, cognizant manner.

It is therefore necessary to learn how to go out in the astral body at will, to see, hear, feel the great realities of life and death.

Some time ago in the suprasensible worlds, I found a certain subject who in life had studied gnosis. With great pain I was able to verify the crude reality that this man was sleeping. I fully realized that he had not managed to manufacture the astral body in his life. I invited him to reflect. I told him, "Friend, you are dead, your body is in the pantheon." He didn't believe me. "Friend, take a little jump with the intention of floating." He did it, but since he did not float [he did not believe] ...

So, we have to think about it and do it. The work is hard, bitter, and difficult, but not impossible. Yes, it is necessary to carve the stone, the hard rock, until chiseling it. That is essential for in depth self-realization.

No one can do this work for us, no one can replace us.

It is up to each of us to face the hard task of crystallizing the three forces within ourselves, here and now.

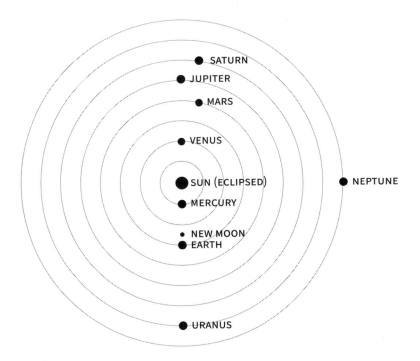

Conjunction of Planets on February 4, 1962

We all know there are small periods of time (months, seasons) in which
nature changes and new influences come into dominance, yet there are
also larger cycles about which humanity has yet to learn. The twelve
months of a calendar year, each marked by a zodiacal sign, mirror
the twelve eras or ages in a Great Year. Each age is 2,140 years long.

On February 4-5, 1962, exactly when there was a new moon AND a
full solar eclipse, there was also an extraordinary celestial conjunction
of the seven primary planets with the Earth. The Sun, the Moon,
Mercury, Venus, Mars, Jupiter, and Saturn were all visibly grouped
close together, and their orbits were aligned with the Earth. This
event signaled a change of era, similar to how the hands of a clock
move into a new day. The Earth had completed an era under the
influence of Pisces, and then entered an era influenced by Aquarius.

The Aquarian Age
A Lecture Given by Samael Aun Weor

We are really doing a gigantic task, which is to start the new Aquarian age within the august thunder of thought...

Brothers and sisters, I want you to fully comprehend what the era of the Aquarius is, and that you base yourselves on concrete, practical, and definitive facts.

You need to remember February 4, 1962, between 2 and 3 in the afternoon.

At that time, all the telescopes in the world were able to see the great planetary cosmic congress, with which the era of the Aquarius really began. Then, the planets of our solar system, gathered in a supreme council in the constellation of Aquarius, originated this new era that will develop more and more in the future.

These are facts that we cannot ignore and that no serious astronomer failed to observe on that date. I don't know why some people, from this or that organization, point to completely different dates for the beginning of the era of Aquarius. We, the Gnostics, are one hundred percent practical and we like to document our affirmations with concrete, reliable, and definitive facts.

The meaning of the new age of the Aquarius is "to know."

If we study this constellation in depth, we will see that it is governed by Uranus[1] and Saturn. Uranus is tremendously explosive and revolutionary in nature; that is why the era of the water bearer will be truly marvelous. Uranus governs the sexual glands, and this is known by any astrologer-scientist.

Undoubtedly, my dear brothers and sisters, the era of the Aquarius is absolutely sexual...

---

1   Greek Οὐρανος, Ouranos (Uranus), "sky, heaven," from Chaldean for Ur = "fire," Anas = "water." The planet that rules sexuality. Οὐρανός has etymological roots in Sanskrit वर्ष varsá 'rain, cloud, shower', Greek eérsē 'dew'. This reveals the role of Uranus / Ouranos influencing our sacred waters, the sexual power, and shines light on many symbols, such as the symbol of dew in the Bible.

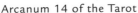
Temperance

Arcanum 14 of the Tarot

Hebe (Greek)
Serving the ambrosia that gives immortality

The time has come to comprehend that symbol of the Aquarius, that symbol of the water carrier who tries to mix the red and white elixirs in a pitcher. In the age of the Aquarius we have to learn to handle the waters of life, the "ens-seminis" as Philippus Theophrastus Bombastus von Hohenheim (Aureolus Paracelsus) wisely said: Remember that within the ens seminis,[2] that is, within the entity of the semen,[3] there is all the ens virtutis[4] of fire.

The Aquarius era is revolutionary and amazing. In this era, all the veils that cover the mysteries of sex will have to be

---

2   Latin "the entity of semen."

3   Semen is Latin, literally "seed of plants, animals, or people; race, inborn characteristic; posterity, progeny, offspring," figuratively "origin, essence, principle, cause." In other words, semen is not just a fluid in masculine bodies. Semen refers to the sexual energy of any creature or entity. In Gnosis, "semen" is a term used for the sexual energy of both masculine and feminine bodies.

4   Latin ens is "entity" and virtutis is "strength/power; courage/bravery; worth/manliness/virtue/character/excellence." Virtutis is derived from Latin vir, "man." So, we can translate this as "power entity." Paracelsus stated that the ens virtutis must be extracted from the ens seminis, thus saying that all virtue and excellence is developed from the force within the sexual waters.

completely removed. In this era, we will have to learn to transmute sexual energy. It is necessary to understand the need for
the transmutation and sublimation of the libido.

The age of Aquarius turns away from vain intellectualism
and enters by a different path. Remember, brothers and sisters, that phrase of the divine rabbi of Galilee, written, by the
way, in the gospel:

> *"No one can serve two masters; for either he will hate
> the one and love the other, or else he will be loyal to the
> one and despise the other. You cannot serve God and
> mammon."* —Matthew 6:24

Mammon[5] is intellect and money. With the beginning of
the age of Aquarius a total revolution arises against intellectualism and against the riches of mammon.

The Wave of Dionysus

Since this luminous era began [1962], the Dionysian wave
vibrates intensely (throughout nature). The Dionysian wave is
extraordinary! Unfortunately, not all of humanity is prepared
to know how to positively polarize with the Dionysian wave;
most have polarized negatively and fatally.

For your better comprehension, I must remind you that
there are currently two international movements that we
could say typify the two aspects of this Dionysian wave. I
refer, emphatically, to the international, universal Gnostic
movement, and to that other (sadly famous) known by the
name of the hippie movement.[6]

---

5   Late Latin mammona, from Greek mamonas, from Aramaic mamona,
    mamon "riches, gain." This word was left untranslated in the Greek
    New Testament (e.g. Matt. vi:24, Luke xvi:9-13) and was retained in the
    Latin Vulgate; thereafter it was mistakenly thought by medieval Chris-
    tians to be the name of a demon.
6   The hippie movement initiated the development of all popular culture
    today; every wave of trends in music, fashion, spirituality, etc is root-
    ed in the hippie movement of the sixties: "free love," concern for the
    environment, rebellion against the previous generation, interest in yoga,
    tantra, and meditation, experimentation with sex, drugs, psychotropics,
    and consciousness-altering devices, etc.

Dionysus (center) accompanied by a satyr and
maenad. Note his staff/spear and cup.

(Greek) Διονυσο, Dionysos, from dio, "god," and nusa, "tree," thus the name literally
means "god of the tree." Also called Bacchus ("riotous"). Originally, Dionysus was
a Greek symbol in the secret mystical schools, and was related to sexual power and
to wine in the same way that Jesus is related to wine in Christianity. Those traditions
were dedicated to purity of character and the perfection of the human being by
transforming the base animal desires into purified spiritual exaltation. Dionysus
was related to the spiritual intoxication that resulted from the purification of the
heart and mind, thus he and his followers were represented in states of ecstasy
(samadhi), dancing, "drunk" on the "wine" of transmutation, like Sufis. Later,
through degeneration, the symbolism of Dionysus was corrupted, and became the
justification for indulgence in desire. Dionysus was represented as androgynous
(having both masculine and feminine aspects, as in the Hebrew word Elohim).
This also was later seized upon as a justification for degenerated interests.

"In the Anacalypsis, Godfrey Higgins conclusively establishes Bacchus (Dionysos)
as one of the early pagan forms of the Christos myth, 'The birthplace of Bacchus,
called Sabazius or Sabaoth, was claimed by several places in Greece; but on Mount
Zelmisus, in Thrace, his worship seems to have been chiefly celebrated. He was
born of a virgin on the 25th of December; he performed great miracles for the
good of mankind; particularly one in which he changed water into wine; he rode
in a triumphal procession on an ass; he was put to death by the Titans, and rose
again from the dead on the 25th of March: he was always called the Saviour. In his
mysteries, he was shown to the people, as an infant is by the Christians at this day, on
Christmas Day morning in Rome.'" —Manly P. Hall, The Secret Teachings of All Ages
Thus, originally, Dionysus represented the way towards elevation of the human being.
However, people inverted the meanings of the symbols in order to justify degeneration.

The positive pole of Dionysus is represented by gnosis, by the Gnostic movement; the negative pole is represented by the hippie movement [and its descendants].

The positive pole of the Dionysian wave is transmutation of the genetic libido, sexual sublimation, mystical ecstasy, divine music, renunciation of the vain intellectualism of mammon and worldly riches (vain and fleeting), of the same tenebrous mammon.

The hippie movement (antithesis of the Gnostic movement), has also renounced the vain intellectualism of mammon and its riches, however, not having been able to polarize positively with the Dionysian wave, it has gone with the negative current: instead of transmuting sexual libido, has preferred the degeneration of sex, vices against nature, promiscuity, etc., and instead of meditation (with its samadhi and its ineffable ecstasy), they favor drugs (cocaine, morphine, marijuana, etc.) And it is through the latter that they unfortunately enter the sublunar regions of nature.[7]

See then, brothers and sisters, those two poles of the Dionysian wave that now vibrate intensely, since the luminous era of Aquarius began...

It would be absurd to renounce the mysteries of sex; it would be absurd to pronounce ourselves against sex yoga with its famous Sahaja Maithuna,[8] because in the age of Aquarius the mysteries of sex must be unveiled, since Ouranos (Uranus, the first great sexual revealer, the lord of the great Atlantis) governs that constellation at this time. It would not be possible to consider ourselves true revolutionaries of Aquarius if

---

7   Their drugs produce visions and experiences, but through the consciousness that is trapped in pride, lust, anger, envy, etc.

8   Sanskrit सहज sahaja, "original, natural," मैथुन maithuna, "marriage, sacramental intercourse, a pair or one of each sex." A reference to superior sexuality in which the orgasm is abandoned and lust is replaced by love.

we made the mistake of repudiating sex yoga, or if, unfortunately, we continued down the path of animal fornication.[9]

It is necessary to comprehend, my dear brothers and sisters, that we are all children of a man and a woman. If we look for the origin of our existence, if we try to know the roots of our life, we discover at its base a man and woman in copulation.

Sex is the origin of life. We are not children of any theory, we are not children of any library, we are not children of this or that institution. Truly, we are children of sex.

Obviously, that energy that put us on the table of existence is the only one that can radically transform us. It is clear that if that energy was capable of giving us life, of creating us, unquestionably it can also transform us and lead us to the intimate self-realization of the Being.

It wasn't theories that created us, it wasn't hypotheses, it wasn't concepts, it wasn't reasoning, but sex. From there we become: from copulation. Behold the very root of our life...

What is interesting, then, is knowing these mysteries of sex, learning to handle that subtle energy that gave us life and to recreate ourselves; that is, regenerate ourselves with it, and through it really transform ourselves; that is the vital, the cardinal, the definitive.

If we repudiate the mysteries of sex, we would, in fact, repudiate the Holy Spirit,[10] the Third Logos.[11] If we said that sex is animal, brutal, materialistic, etc., we would blaspheme against the Holy Spirit. Let us remember that sexual energy is the

---

9   The misuse of sexual energy in any form. The original sin. The etymological root of fornication means "to burn." In esoteric tradition, fire is a symbol of sexual energy; those who fornicate are 'burned' (tortured) by their own uncontrolled sexual fires: physical and psychological suffering. Fornication leads to the sleeping of consciousness and development of the ego. See glossary.

10 The Christian name for the third aspect of the Holy Trinity, or "God." On the Kabbalistic Tree of Life, this is the third sephirah, called Binah, "intelligence." This force has many names in other religions, such as Shiva in Hinduism, Nirmanakaya in Buddhism. "The Holy Spirit is the Fire of Pentecost or the fire of the Holy Spirit called Kundalini by the Hindus..." —Samael Aun Weor, *The Perfect Matrimony*

11 The aspect of the universal trinity that creates life, which is always through sex. See Logos in the glossary.

wonderful living expression of the Third Logos, which creates and always creates anew.

Instead of spitting our slanderous slime into the sanctum sanctorum[12] of the sexual mysteries, we should study them deeply, sincerely.

It is necessary to learn to look at sex with deep veneration. Unfortunately, people have morbid minds, and always see sex with the eyes of the devil. They are not capable of perceiving the sanctity of the Third Logos...

The Holy Grail and Spear

Let us remember the Holy Grail, the one that Melchizedek delivered to Abraham. They say that this patriarch officiated, precisely, in the presence of Melchizedek, with the Holy Grail.

Ancient allegories say that the Holy Grail was in Noah's ark; some affirm that it came into the hands of the queen of Sheba and that after submitting him to multiple tests she handed it over to Solomon...

Ancient esotericism affirms that at the Last Supper Jesus drank the sacred wine from that marvelous chalice.

They say that Joseph of Arimathea, the great Roman senator, collected in the divine cup the blood that flowed from the stigmata of the beloved savior of the world... There are those who affirm that this holy man, after having filled the chalice with that precious, divine liquor, hid it together with the famous spear of Longinus, underground and in his house... When the Roman police searched for the chalice, they demanded that Joseph of Arimathea return it because it belonged to the temple, but the old Roman senator did not want to deliver it; for this reason, my dear brothers and sisters, he had to be taken prisoner.

But when that distinguished man came out of jail, he looked for the chalice and the spear and with them he went to Rome in search of Christians. On reaching that ancient city, he found persecution against the Christians. He then

---

12 Latin sanctum sanctorum is a translation of the Hebrew קֹדֶשׁ הַקֳּדָשִׁים, "Holy of Holies," the holiest place in the Tabernacle.

Titurel, former leader of
the Grail Knights, with
the Grail and Holy Spear,
from Wagner's Parsifal.

continued on his way along the shores of the Mediterranean,
and they say that one night an angel appeared to him in a
dream and told him, "That chalice has great magnetic power,
because it contains the blood of the redeemer of the world.
Bury it there..." and showed him the mountain of Montserrat,
in Catalonia, Spain. And it was there, in that transcendent
Monsalvat, where the Roman man hid those precious trea-
sures, the chalice and the spear.

Brothers and sisters, I want you to comprehend the profound significance of those relics. The chalice represents
the feminine yoni, the woman's sexual organ, and the spear,
the one with which Longinus wounded the Lord's side, the
same one with which Parsifal healed the wound in the side of
Amfortas, is the living emblem of sexual force. It clearly represents the phallus, the masculine virile principle. So, brothers and sisters, the chalice and in the spear are the key to all
power...

The Great Arcanum

The time has come to know that it is not possible to transform ourselves with a force other than the one that created
us, that put us on the mat of existence. It is urgent to under-

stand that only the marvelous force of Eros can really transform us intimately in a definitive way.

Many have talked about the Kundalini,[13] the igneous serpent of our magical powers; however, it is not possible to
wake her without knowing the key. Obviously, that key is the
Great Arcanum, it is sex yoga, the Sahaja Maithuna.

When we touch on these mysteries of sex, when we quote
them, the Puritans are horrified, they consider us "sex fanat-
ics," ignoring that the Gnostic studies have very solid founda-
tions.

In former times, the one who dare to divulged the Great
Arcanum[14] was sentenced to death: his head was cut off, his
heart was ripped out and his ashes were thrown to the four
winds... something similar happened in Aztec Mexico. In any
case, I want you to know, my dear brothers and sisters, that
the Great Arcanum is the Maithuna, Sexual Magic.

I have given the key in my books: connection of the lin-
gam-yoni[15] without releasing the ens seminis; the mantra:
I.A.O. (This is the fundamental mantra). There are many others that are used in the Maithuna and with great pleasure I
will show them to you later...

I want you to know that the Sahaja Maithuna can only
be practiced with the priest-husband and priestess-wife; the
Sahaja Maithuna should not be practiced with different people;[16] the Sahaja Maithuna, only and exclusively, is lawful to
practice between husband and wife, in legitimately constituted homes.

---

13 Sanskrit कुण्डलिनी, the power of the Divine Mother that awakens in those
    who earn it.

14 (Latin. plural: arcana). A secret, a mystery. The root of the term "ark" as
    in the Ark of Noah and the Ark of the Covenent.

15 Sanskrit लिङ्ग male sexual organ, also "sign, mark, proof evidence." San-
    skrit योनी, female sexual organ.

16 "Commit no adultery. This law is broken by even looking at the wife of
    another with a lustful mind." —Buddha

Seven Primary Chakras on the Spinal Column

The Fire of Kundalini

After some time of incessant practices, without ever spilling the cup of Hermes, that is, without releasing the ens seminis, the igneous serpent of our magical powers awakens within the coccygeal chakra[17] to begin its inward and upward journey along the spinal cord canal. Obviously, as the sexual fire of the kundalini begins its ascension, as it advances, it opens the different chakras along the spine.

The first center that opens is in the coccyx and is known in the East by the name Muladhara, and in the West in the Apocalypse (Revelation of St John) by the name church of Ephesus. It is a beautiful lotus flower in the coccygeal bone; it has four wonderful petals. It is the fundamental center. It gives us power over the gnomes[18] of the earth and over the tattva prithvi, that is, over the petrous ether that exists throughout planet Earth.

When the igneous serpent of our magical powers ascending through the spinal cord canal reaches the level of the prostate or uterus, the second church opens, the church of Smyrna, the famous Svadhishthana chakra, the extraordinary lotus with the six petals that gives power over the waters of life, over the tattva apas, over the undines[19] of nature.

When the ascending igneous serpent of our magical powers reaches the height of the solar plexus, then the church of Pergamus opens; this is a beautiful lotus flower with ten petals. It gives us power over the tattva tejas[20] and over salamanders;[21] it confers on us telepathy, the power to capture the thoughts of people at a distance, the power over the universal fire of life, etc.

---

17 Sanskrit चक्र "wheel, circle." In Asian traditions, the word chakra refers to any wheel or circle, and is often used to describe circular weapons used by the gods. Most people today associate the word with subtle centers of energetic transformation that are within our bodies. There are hundreds of chakras in our multi-dimensional physiology, but seven primary ones related to the awakening of consciousness.

18 Elementals related to the earth element. See glossary.

19 Elementals related to the water element. See glossary.

20 The subtle source of fire.

21 Elementals related to the fire element. See glossary.

When the divine fire reaches the height of the heart, the church of Thyatira opens, the lotus flower with twelve petals, the famous Anahata chakra. The development of that faculty allows us to put our physical body within the fourth dimension;[22] astral projections become simple and easy, etc.

When the sacred fire reaches the creative larynx, we can create anything with the imagination and crystallize it through the word. The throat chakra is the church of Sardis, which has sixteen splendid petals; it gives us clairaudience, that is, the magical ear, the ability to hear the voices of the ultra. It also gives us conceptual synthesis, etc...

When the sacred fire reaches the height of the eyebrows, then the famous "lotus" of the two petals opens, the church of Philadelphia, the eye of clairvoyance.

And when the sacred fire reaches the pineal gland, the Sahasrara chakra opens, the "lotus" with 1,000 petals, the church of Laodicea. It is there where the divine fire, the sacred fire of the Divine Mother Kundalini marries Lord Shiva; that is, with the Holy Spirit, with the Third Logos (Binah). In those moments, the famous Shiva-shakti tattva vibrates intensively.

That is how the sacred fire opens the seven churches of the Apocalypse of Saint John...

Summarizing, we will say:

- The first church that opens is the church of Ephesus, the Muladhara chakra
- The second, the Svadhishthana, the church of Smyrna
- The third is the church of Pergamus, the Manipura chakra
- The fourth is the church of Thyatira, Anahata chakra
- The fifth is the church of Sardis, Vishuddha chakra
- The sixth is the church of Philadelphia, Ajna
- Lastly, the church of Laodicea, Sahasrara.

These seven chakras give us immense powers:

---

22 Also called Jinn science. Read *The Yellow Book* by Samael Aun Weor.

- The first gives us power over the earth element
- The second over the water element
- The third over the fire element
- The fourth over air
- The fifth gives us power over the pure akasha so we can keep our body alive, even during the deep nights of the great pralaya
- The sixth gives us clairvoyance, the power to see the thoughts of others as in an open book, the power to see the supersensible worlds, to study the mysteries of life and death, etc.
- The seventh gives us the power of polyvoyance, the ability to study the akashic records of nature; the dangma eye, the diamond eye, the divine eye that gives us deep inner illumination.

These seven chakras make us, in fact, kings and queens, priests and priestesses of nature, according to the order of Melchizedek, king of Salem.

These seven chakras, brothers and sisters, open with the sacred fire of kundalini.

Awakening the Kundalini

It is an absurd thing to affirm that "the awakening of the kundalini is dangerous." I want you to know, my dear brothers and sisters, that no neophyte is alone in this work. Everyone who works in the ninth sphere, that is, in sex, everyone who works in the forge of the Cyclops, is undoubtedly assisted. The brothers and sisters of the esoteric brotherhood watch over the one who works with the mysteries of fire. None of you will be alone in this work; the igneous serpent is led by the brothers and sisters of the secret fraternity, along the spinal medullary canal.

However, it is good to know, my dear brothers and sisters, that this kind of work is not done overnight; in all this there are efforts and efforts.

The Faithful Apostles Receive the Sacred Fire

"And suddenly there came a sound from heaven as of a rushing
mighty wind, and it filled all the house where they were sitting.
And there appeared unto them cloven tongues like as of fire,
and it sat upon each of them. And they were all filled with the
Holy Ghost [the Third Logos]..." —Christian Bible, Acts 2

The disciple must not let oneself fall, because the disciple who lets oneself fall has to fight a lot later to recover what was lost. The one who ejaculates the ens seminis loses the fire...

In the spinal cord there are 33 vertebrae that are closely related to the 33 degrees of occult Masonry. As we practice the Sahaja Maithuna, the sacred fire ascends slowly, from vertebra to vertebra, that is, from degree to degree. When we make the mistake of releasing the semen, then the fire descends one or more vertebrae, depending on the magnitude of the fault.

I want you to know, my dear brothers and sisters, that the sacred fire of the Kundalini only awakens with the charms of love.

Some suppose that it is possible to arouse that fire through pranayama or other Hatha yoga exercises, but these are nothing more than sincerely mistaken people; they affirm what they do not know. Remember that "the road that leads to the abyss is paved with good intentions..." What happens is that many who practice pranayama manage the rise of some igneous sparks (sparks that are released from the flame, sparks that jump and circulate from the bonfire), and then they believe that they have awakened the fire. Obviously, each of these sparks produce awakenings of the consciousness, they produce illumination, but that is not the complete awakening of the igneous serpent of our magical powers. Although it is true that any fraction of the kundalini (no matter how small) produces interior illuminations, increases in the consciousness, it is also no less true that pranayama does not achieve the total awakening of all the sacred fire; that is obvious.

Only through the charms of love does the divine serpent kundalini awaken, to begin its ascension along the spinal cord canal and truly lead us to the intimate self-realization of the Being. Awakening the kundalini is not dangerous, because everyone who is working on it is assisted by the masters of the white universal brotherhood...

I want you to be practical, to transform yourselves, really, through love. Only by loving can we achieve the intimate transformation of the Being. Only by loving can we fully achieve self-realization. Only by learning how to handle that creative energy of the Third Logos can we reach the final liberation.

To say there is danger in the awakening of the kundalini, that it can go through other paths, etc. is false, because those who awaken the fire are always assisted.

Those who suppose that the sacred fire can awaken instantly, reaching the head ipso facto, immediately, are lying, because really the sacred fire goes up little by little through the dorsal spine, according to the merits of the heart.

Remember that each of the 33 vertebrae of the dorsal spine implies certain virtues. No one could achieve the ascent of fire, for example in the 12th vertebra, if he does not have the moral conditions of that vertebra. No one could take the sacred fire to the 20th vertebra, if she does not fulfill all the conditions and requirements of that vertebra. Thus, for the sacred fire to rise to this or that vertebra, it is necessary that we possess the virtues corresponding to it. That is why through the 33 vertebrae we have to suffer a lot and go through innumerable tests.

This is the teaching of fire, my dear brothers and sisters. This is the only way you can become omnipotent gods, with powers over fire, air, water, and earth. This is not a question of theories, my dear brothers and sisters, this is a matter of concrete and definitive facts.

The time has come for you to free yourselves from vain intellectualism. The moment has arrived in which you understand the mysteries of sex. The time has come for you to definitively descend to the ninth sphere, to work intensely in the burning forge of Vulcan.[23]

It is urgent, my dear brothers and sisters, that you get rid of many prejudices that impede progress. It is necessary that

---

23 The Latin or Roman name for the Greek god Ἥφαιστος Hephaestus known by the Egyptians as Ptah. A god of fire with a deep and ancient mythology, commonly remembered as the blacksmith who forges weapons for gods and heroes. Vulcan is very important in the tradition of Alchemy. In Hinduism, he is symbolized by Tvastri, later called Visvakarma.

you, my dear brothers and sisters, put aside the fear-mongers, ignorant people who tell you that "awakening the kundalini is dangerous," ignorant people who tell you that "sexual magic is harmful," etc... All this is false, my dear brothers and sisters, because the adepts of the universal white fraternity, with which all of us initiates are in contact, have self-realized through sexual magic.

In the Gnostic movement there are millions of brothers and sisters who work with the Sahaja Maithuna, and none have gone mad, none are sick, all enjoy perfect health.

If someone tells you that sexual magic is harmful, tell him that he is lying, because in the Gnostic movement there are millions of brothers and sisters who thoroughly know the mysteries of sex. There are millions of brothers and sisters who practice sexual magic, and none of them are crazy.

There are also, in the East, millions of Gnostic brothers and sisters who work with the Sahaja Maithuna, and in Europe, there are Gnostic schools where the brothers and sisters also dedicate themselves to the study of the sacred mysteries of sex: all of them enjoy full health.

Reflect on these words, brothers and sisters. I do not want, in this lecture, to go deeper. I only want to go into the prologue of our studies. Later, in the future, I will teach you, little by little, all the mysteries related to sex. For now, my dear brothers and sisters, listen to what I say to you, longing for your inner progress.

The Immaculate Conception
by Giovanni Battista Tiepolo

The Divine Mother Kundalini crushes
the Kundabuffer under her feet.

Our True Mother
A Lecture Given by Samael Aun Weor

Brothers and sisters, this is the moment to understand the intimate relationship between death and life.

We have been wisely told that the path of life is formed by the hoof prints of death's horse, and that is certainly a tremendous truth. When we die, we find that the extremes meet; we depart from our family, ancestors and relatives, and we believe everything will be forgotten through time and distance, but when we die, we return again to their bosom. This is something that is unclear and incoherent for us. I do not want to say that we return immediately, but eventually, since it is obvious that between death and the new birth there are post-mortem states; however, I repeat, after death, after the well-known post-mortem states, we return to the bosom of our ancestors and relatives.

It could be objected that a long time could have passed and they would have died, and that is right, but they in turn have returned to the bosom of their ancestors, as the ancestors have returned to the bosom of their ancestors, and thus they form a chain, so that when we return, we will find them dressed in new bodies. The same family groups always develop from life to life. They can, indeed, change the roles a bit: if we were children before, then later we will be the parents. The sexes also change—that depends on the karma of each one. But family groups always come together to repeat the same episodes. That is the law of recurrence.

There are also groups that, although they are not family, meet again to determine historical moments of humanity. One very famous group was that of the French Revolution: Marie Antoinette, Marat, Robespierre, Danton, etc. I set out to investigate this group, and despite the slander raised against Marie Antoinette, I found her in a white tunic. She is a very chaste woman, despite the fact that she was accused of being an adulteress. Also within the group is Marat, an initiate who at certain times in history had certain very tough missions.

Archduchess Maria Antonia of Austria in 1772, at the age of 16 years, who later became Queen Marie Antoinette of France. Painted by Joseph Kranzinger.

And Robespierre, who appears as antagonistic, as the antithesis of Marie Antoinette and the aristocratic group, is also part of it. That group fulfills specific missions that are very tragic on the path of history. That group is currently disincarnated. In the superior worlds, these people always walk together. The day they take shape is the start of another kind of revolution like the one that took place in France. There is no doubt that they are a class of beings who work hard and suffer with drastic, terrible missions. Marie Antoinette amazes with her courage. She is impassive in the superior worlds, dressed in her white tunic. She is a true heroine in the most transcendental sense of the word, a woman capable of making great sacrifices for humanity, who made mistakes, I cannot deny it, but not as much as her slanderers suppose.

Thus, this humanity marches and forms in groups. Those of us present here have also been gathered in groups and we have met incessantly, that is obvious. This same group working now was also gathered before the Porfiriato revolution (1876), back in the last century, and now we are together again. I have recognized my friends, I have spoken to them, but they do not remember. Sometimes I am even glad they do not remember, because since I was a fallen bodhisattva, I even committed or caused some harm to them.

Awakened consciousness accompanies me, yes, thank God. For me, at the end of an existence it is like a masked ball, the masks fall and the harsh reality is revealed. In any case, I speak to the consciousness, and whoever knows how to understand, well, understand.

I want the brothers and sisters here to wake up, so that you will know how terrible this law of recurrence is. To all those present here, I know them well... There I see the lawyer. There I see Rafael Ruiz Ochoa who accompanies me on all the paths of God. Here I see Susana, who is now Clarita... But they don't remember me, so waking up is something very essential, very necessary. What does one do all their lives with their consciousness asleep? Nothing! That is very sad.

But I tell you, my dear brothers and sisters, that life and death are intimately related. No matter how far you have gone from the company of your ancestors, from your relatives, you will return to their bosom. Sometimes one says certain things... For example, sometimes one takes a body here, and at other times one has to be born in France, England, or Germany. It could be asked, what am I going to do there, if I don't have relatives there? Yes, you have relatives there from other existences. Part of the Old Testament speaks about the death of Solomon, and it is said, "I will gather you into my people." I don't remember if it was Solomon or one of those great kings of antiquity, but that is a tremendous reality, a tremendous truth. That is why we cannot in any way behave badly with our relatives, with our folks, or with our families, because undoubtedly, we are united to them by blood ties, and sooner or later we have to return to them. We must by all possible means try to behave as best as possible.

> "For I will take you from among the heathen, and gather you out of all countries, and will bring you into your own land. Then will I sprinkle clean water upon you, and ye shall be clean: from all your filthiness, and from all your idols, will I cleanse you. A new heart also will I give you, and a new spirit will I put within you: and I will take away the stony heart out of your flesh, and I will give you an heart of flesh. And I will put my spirit within you, and cause you to walk in my statutes, and ye shall keep my judgments, and do them. And ye shall dwell in the land that I gave to your fathers; and ye shall be my people, and I will be your God."
> —Ezekiel 36:24-28

Theories and the Intellect

The crude reality of life certainly distances itself from vain intellectualism. One can have many theories in one's mind, but they are useless. The only thing that truly serves is what is connected by blood. Friedrich Nietzsche said for a reason:

> "Of all that is written, I love only what a person hath written with his blood. Write with blood, and thou wilt find that blood is spirit... He that writeth in blood and

proverbs doth not want to be read, but learnt by heart."
—Friedrich Nietzsche, Thus Spoke Zarathustra

When the famous Faust tries to sign a pact with Mephistopheles, he wanted to write with ink and Mephistopheles tells him,

"And to sign thy name thou'lt take a drop of blood...
Blood is a juice of rarest quality." —Faust, Johann Wolfgang von Goethe

That is a tremendous truth! The blood has a magical, intense, tremendous power.

I have been able to see in practice that vain intellectualisms are of no use. Once, I was talking with my Divine Mother Kundalini in a great room. I embraced her with love, that of son to mother. Afterwards, when she sat down, she seemed to me like an ineffable Madonna,[1] and I asked her the questions that you already know, such as if it is possible that there is someone in the physical world who can self-realize without the need for Sexual Magic, "Impossible, that is not possible." After my Divine Mother Kundalini got up from that chair, a pedant of the intellect, one of the sons of Mammon, approached her and asked her a completely intellectual question, with very difficult conclusions that I myself did not understand, to which My Divine Mother Kundalini did not give an answer. She simply turned away and withdrew. For Her, that has no value. The only thing that has value for the Divine Mother is authentic wisdom and perfect love.

Where to Find Wisdom

We must value all of life's experiences, not underestimating family experiences, nor underestimating experiences in the city, or at work, because it turns out that from those experiences the summum[2] of wisdom is obtained. For example, I extract wisdom from the experiences of life itself. Any scene, any event in the daily bustle of existence, helps me to obtain

---

1   Italian, "my lady," to indicate the Virgin Mary or any morally pure and chaste woman.
2   Latin "greatest, highest"

wisdom. I simply use meditation. During meditation I try to extract the deep significance of any experience of life, practical life, of any event of daily living, and by grasping that deep significance it is obvious that I acquire wisdom.

I have come to demonstrate the reality that people do not know how to differentiate what is good from what is bad. They do not have a clear awareness of what is good and what is evil. Oftentimes, when wanting to do good, they do evil. Oftentimes, trying to do evil, they do good. People do not know in themselves. They do not have an awakened consciousness to know what is good and what is bad. The Tree of the Knowledge of Good and Evil should not be despised. In everything good there is something bad. In all the bad, there is some good. If people were aware of what is good and what is bad, there would be wisdom everywhere, but what exists everywhere is ignorance.

Another of the most serious problems is that of interpretation. We are in a true Tower of Babel, where no one understands anyone. How often does one speak certain words and they are misinterpreted? The serious thing is that those who often misunderstand feel offended, when the person who said it had no intention of offending anyone, and it is because everyone has ego inside, and it is a lousy secretary who misinterprets, disfigures everything, gives words another meaning. Knowing how to listen is quite difficult, brothers and sisters, because that secretary that every human being carries inside misinterprets everything, translates according to its prejudices, preconceptions, opinions, and that is where the problem lies. Conclusion: we are surrounded by things that we underestimated that are worth a lot. We often underestimate our relatives, and that is a serious mistake, because we have to return to them.

Death and life are intimately related. We underestimate the small details of daily life, the small events, when we can extract the maximum wisdom from them. We look for wisdom in theories but there is none, and where it is we do not look for it. It is obvious that wisdom must be found in the chores of daily life, in the struggle for daily bread, in living with our own, with our relatives. One must know how to find wisdom by not underestimating experiences, extracting content from them through the technique of meditation.

Behold the difference between Dionysus and Mammon! Dionysus is not intellectual nor is he interested in intellect; he is not greedy either, he renounces wealth. Mammon is one hundred percent intellectual, and wants material goods, wealth, money, at all costs. Dionysus and Mammon are therefore antithetical.

We who have renounced the current of Mammon have become polarized with Dionysus. As we told you previously, not everyone has been able to polarize with Dionysus. The hippies, for example, are polarized with the negative aspect of Dionysus; they renounced Mammon, yes, but they did not know how to polarize themselves positively with Dionysus, but rather negatively; instead of transmuting creative energy as we, Dionysus' devotees, do, they have fallen into infra-sexuality, into sexual degeneration. Here is the difference. Instead of the mystical ecstasy that we acquire through meditation, they enter the infernal worlds through pills, L.S.D., marijuana, mushrooms, etc.

The Dionysus current is active, but we must polarize ourselves positively. Certainly, the supporters of Dionysus who have polarized in his positively radiant, luminous form, have renounced intellectualism. We are perfectly convinced that it does not lead us to the experience of reality, the truth.

We acquire wisdom through meditation. As the themes for meditation, we choose the experience of daily battles, the event of the moment, the event of the day, the most outstanding, that which intellectuals underestimate, the minuscule facts of domestic life or the kitchen, perhaps the incident on the street, or the encounter with the sweeper or the police, or any fact at the factory or at the office. From there we will extract wisdom through meditation.

It is not just a matter of understanding these daily events. One may have understood and yet not have apprehended, catching their deep significance. What is interesting is catching the deep significance of what we have comprehended.

When one captures that deep significance of what is comprehended, the result is wisdom. Such wisdom, acquired in a practical way and through meditation, is worth more than all the theories of the intellect together.

I was able to appreciate my Divine Mother Kundalini, how she turned her back on that theorist. For Her, theories are worthless. Those complicated and difficult theories are good for Mammon, not for Dionysus' devotees.

In these times, my dear brothers and sisters, it is painful to see how people have overdeveloped their intellects. When I see one of those university students stuffed with theories, I feel compassion for them. What do such intellectuals look like? Simply like a man who has developed a superfluous organ at the expense of others. For example, someone who excessively developed the abdomen, someone who has one arm longer than a shorter one, someone who has one foot larger than the other: a monstrosity! Such a monster is the individual who has exclusively developed the intellect at the expense of the other faculties, a monster developing one part while the others have remained in an embryonic state. Out there are monsters in life, individuals like this who are born with a huge head and small bodies, individuals with huge bodies but legs that are useless for walking, too short. Thus, psychologically speaking, they have developed the intellect at the expense of their other faculties. I believe that all the faculties must develop harmoniously, otherwise we would become psychological monsters. It is not possible to develop all of our faculties harmoniously if we simply fill our heads with theories and more theories.

It seems better to me that we learn to extract the wisdom of the facts of practical life through meditation. That is better than the "hippie" style.

Let us drink the wine of meditation in the cup of perfect concentration. This is how we acquire what is called wisdom.

Theories are useless. At the time of death we forget them, because the only thing we take with us to the superior worlds, beyond the grave, is what we have become as consciousness. We take with us the love of our parents, friends, nephews, relatives, brothers, grandparents, uncles, relatives. We take with us the lived experiences of life in its crude reality. The intellectual theories, the theories that fatten the mind, we do not take them with us, because they do not belong to the consciousness. One can only take the things that belong to consciousness...

Here you could object, "Then the ego? Is the ego from consciousness?" Yes, it is of the consciousness, unfortunately. The ego is the result of mistakes made by the sleeping consciousness, the errors within which the consciousness sleeps. It is obvious that we also take with us the errors of our consciousness. Our egos are the results of errors made by the consciousness. We take with us what has become consciousness, even mistakes [defects and vices]. The theories we learned have nothing to do with consciousness.

Seeing this, brothers and sisters, we need to wake up. For this, it is necessary to live alert and vigilant like a sentry in times of war.

The book of life is the best of all books. True wisdom is from consciousness.

Our True Mother

What would become of us, my dear brothers and sisters, if at the time of the death of the ego, of the "I," of myself, we did not have our Divine Mother Kundalini? It is obvious that we would be orphans. Let us take this a little further: by dissolving the ego we remain orphans in this world, because no one understands us, even if we understand others. Nothing attracts us—desires, parties, passions, all that has died for us, life has ended, turned into a desert. One like this can live in a city, yet is alone. If it were not for the Divine Mother Kundalini one would be dead, but fortunately she comforts us. With good reason the Hail Mary says,

> "Pray for us sinners, now and at the hour of our death."

This does not refer to the death of the physical body, but of the ego. She can pray for us at the hour of death. She can ask

Athena / Minerva
Greek symbol of the Divine
Mother. Note her spear and
serpent. Around her neck she
wears the remnants of the
slain Medusa: her antithesis.

the Logos on our behalf. Yes, she can beg. Yes, she can beg in certain White Lodges for us.

The Divine Mother Kundalini is a true mother, a mother in the fullest sense of the word, our authentic Eternal Mother.

Thus, so long as one kills the ego, there is no need to fear.

How does one remain if one eliminates it, without ego, without "I"? (This is how some protest.) One is not left alone. Inside, one is fortified, consoled. The igneous serpent of our magical powers, Kundalini Shakti, comforts and helps us. Thus, thanks to her, no one is defenseless.

She in herself has wisdom, love, and power...

Wisdom that is not of the mind, since she is beyond the mind...

Limitless love and power over all that is, has been, and will be...

The Source of Power

But you see, the igneous serpent of our magical powers is not in any theory, it is in sex, in the very root of sex, in the very root of that force that put us into existence, in the depths of our consciousness.

Many others who have written about the Kundalini present it to us as something cold, awakened by the "bellows" system: "inhale through the right nostril, exhale through the left nostril." This is the error of the theorists who have not experienced that fire in themselves! It turns out that this fire that rises through the spinal canal, that flame, is not something frozen like a theory that freezes in the brain, no, it is the fire of love, the fire of sexual delight wisely understood, the flame of Eros[3] that ascends victorious after being awakened

---

3   (Greek Ερως, Roman Cupid, Amor) An ancient Greek symbol of love related to the fundamental force of existence (love, sex). Sadly, as with most esoteric symbols, the interpretation and depiction of Eros was perverted over time. "Eros was one of the fundamental causes in the formation of the world, inasmuch as he was the uniting power of love, which brought order and harmony among the conflicting elements of which Chaos consisted." —Dictionary of Greek and Roman Biography and Mythology

CROWN	I (EE)
FRONTAL	I (EE)
THROAT	E (EH)
HEART	O (OH)
PULMONARY	A (AH)
SOLAR PLEXUS	U (UU)
PROSTATE / UTERUS	M (MM)
ROOT	S (SS)

Seven Primary Chakras on the Spinal Column

by means of sacred copulation. That flame can and does open
the seven churches of the Apocalypse of Saint John. They
are the seven magnetic centers placed exactly in the cardinal
points of the human being.

The first church of Ephesus is in the coccyx, with its corresponding plexus between the creative organs and the anus.
See the intimacy of that chakra or plexus...

And the second center, the prostate/uterus, how great it is!
Who would have thought that wonders exist in the prostate/
uterus, however there are, yes. While the first church gives
us power over the Prithvi tattva, over the gnomes that popu-
late the face of the Earth, the second gives us power over the
waters of life.

And what shall we say of the third church that is in the
umbilical region? That of acquiring power over the sacred
fire, power over volcanoes.

And what shall we say about the fourth church of Thyatira
that gives us power over the air, over hurricanes, over storms?
We are not going to acquire powers through ambiguous talk,
or through confusing intellectual terms, but by loving with all
our hearts, developing in us the highest, purest feeling, raising
the sacred flame of love to that marvelous chakra. It is obvious that such a center gives us the power to enter and leave
the body whenever we want, such as being able to put the
physical body in a Jinn state, such as being able to command
hurricanes and storms, that is obvious. See how the flame of
love can perform those miracles in oneself and within oneself
here and now!

We talked a little about conceptual synthesis... There are
very few people who actually have the power to synthesize;
there are people who to tell the truth have to write a huge
volume. It really would not be possible to acquire it without
the development of the throat chakra. This chakra is not
going to open through voluminous texts, nor by engaging
in lustful topics, nor by getting into universities, but by
raising the delicious fire of sexual bliss to the creative larynx. Unquestionably, among other things, it also gives us

the power of clairaudience, the power to hear in the internal worlds.

And let us now think of the frontal chakra, a resplendent chakra that allows us to see the mysteries of life and death, the ultra of things, which allows us to see everything that has been and will be, allows us to study the hidden anatomy, etc. It is not acquired by reading, but by raising the fire of love to the brain, which corresponds to the cavernous center in the cerebellum.

A little further on we reach the pineal gland, the crown of the saints, that splendid faculty, that marvelous chakra that allows us to study the Akashic Records of Nature. It really opens raising the sacred fire, then it turns resplendent, and the zodiacal belt also shines in it.

How blind is the intellect!

Remember, I have been telling you that our solar system has twelve planets. I did not need huge volumes to find that out. For that, we have higher order faculties. Recently I saw in the newspaper that scientists have discovered a planet that is beyond the orbit of Pluto. Beyond those planets is another...

Before, it was not twelve, but thirteen. You already know that the thirteenth planet exploded, and scientists know that the fragments revolve around the Sun.[4] It was the thirteenth that exploded. So now we have twelve planets.

It is still debated whether or not there is life on Mars. They have not been able to photograph it. What can be seen as dust storms is water, and it is obvious that there is life, it is inhabited, it has water, which is the basis of life.

In the end, the intellect struggles, while one can investigate faster. The intellect is clumsy. Look how backwards "physics" is, such as these rocket engines, where is the progress? And this is how our scientists from the tower of Babel think, to conquer space without having conquered time? To conquer space, you must first conquer time. You already know that time is the fourth coordinate, the fourth dimension; as long as consciousness has not conquered the fourth dimension, it will uselessly try to conquer infinite space.

---

4   The asteroid belt between Jupiter and Mars.

This new era is different from the past. Now, intuitive individuals will stand out, those who go beyond intellectualism. Now the current of Dionysus will prevail. The theoreticians of intellectualism will be left behind, they will be like museum displays, they will be seen as too clumsy.

In the new era, the intuitive ones will stand out. That is the harsh reality of the facts.

We all have to adjust more and more to the new era that is beginning. The bygone era is past. Look at those nuns with vestments from the era of Pisces. They no longer fit in with the time we are in. They look obsolete, out of date.

When the age of the water carrier arrived, everything shook. You see how the religion of Rome tottered, and is still tottering? They are all fighting against other sects, who are also shaken, because Aquarius has a tremendous revolutionary force.

Aquarius is ruled by Uranus and Saturn. Uranus, the main ruler of Aquarius, is completely revolutionary. The curious thing is that Uranus governs the sexual endocrine glands. So the one who wants to accommodate to the vibration of Aquarius but does not enter the path of sexual regeneration is condemning oneself to failure. Uranus is an extraordinarily rebellious planet!

The Dionysian wave has been vibrating since the Sun entered Aquarius. It is the force of Uranus. Along this path of sex, of transmutation, we find the Kundalini, wisdom, intuition. That path displaces the intellect. That path precisely marks the new era as new, and the past as the past.

At this moment the world is completely in turmoil. Certainly, Aquarius has not found humanity properly prepared. Humanity has become negatively polarized with Aquarius.

Since Uranus is naturally explosive, atomic experiments are also intensifying. The abuse of nuclear energy will intensify catastrophes during this Age of Aquarius, because the atom has been abused too much and will continue to be abused, increasingly tremendous bombs will be invented. This is how

it happened with the Atlanteans, they invented tremendous
bombs...

Light
A Lecture Given by Samael Aun Weor

Moses[1] said in Genesis:

"Let there be light, and there was light!"

This is not something that corresponds to a remote past, no! This tremendous beginning, which shuddered at the first instant, never changes time, it is as eternal as all eternity; we must take it as a crude reality from instant to instant, and from moment to moment...

Let us remember Goethe, the great German initiate; before dying his last words were: "light, more light!.."., and he died. (In parentheses, Goethe is now reincarnated in Holland, he has a physical body; but this time, he does not have a male physical body, now he has female physical body, and is married to a Dutch prince; now she is a highborn Dutch lady; that is very interesting, isn't it?)[2]

Well, continuing forward with what we have started, this matter about making light is very important, because as long as one lives in darkness, one yearns for the light; one is blind. The person who is stuck in a sinkhole, in the darkness, in an underground, what he most yearns for is light...

Well, the essence is the most worthy, the most decent thing that we have inside; the essence originally comes from the Milky Way, where the musical note La resonates; then passes to the Sun, with the note Sol, and then comes to this physical world with the note Mi...[3]

The essence is beautiful. It is a fraction of one's human-Christic principle, the human soul, which normally dwells in the causal world. This is why, with just reason, it is

---

1 The Hebrew name Moshe משה is מ Mem, "water," ש Shin "fire," and ה Hei "womb," to literally mean "born of water and fire (spirit)"—in other words, Moses was "born of the water and the Spirit (fire)" just as Jesus explained the Second Birth to Nicodemus. Moses is a Twice-born Master, and also a deep symbol.
2 Read *The Mystery of the Golden Flower* by Samael Aun Weor.
3 Read *Light from Darkness* by Samael Aun Weor.

described as "Christ-essence" or "Christ-consciousness," and it is said that our consciousness in Christ can be saved, etc.

All that is true, all that is correct; but what is serious about our consciousness, about our essence, is that being so precious, possessing such marvelous gifts, such precious natural powers, it is bottled within all those undesirable, subjective elements that we unfortunately carry within. That is to say, it is stuck (speaking in synthesis), within a dungeon...

Our essence wants the light, but how? We yearn for it; there is no one who does not yearn for the light! Unless that one is already too lost. Well, when one has any aspiration, one wants the light... So one has to do it; and this matter about "making light" is very serious matter, because it implies destroying the receptacles or dungeons, or speaking in synthesis, the black den where our essence is stuck, to rescue it, free it, extract it from there, in order for one to remain as one should be, that is, as an enlightened person, as a true "seer," as a true enlightened being, enjoying that fullness that belongs to us by nature and to which we truly have a right.

But it takes heroism, a series of tremendous acts of heroism, to free our soul, to get it out of the dungeon where it is stuck, to steal it from the darkness.

It would be interesting for you to truly cognizantly comprehend what I am saying. It could even be the case that even though you are listening, you do not hear, or do not live the meanings of the words that I am saying. You have to know how to value these words, to understand what I am affirming...

Rescuing the soul, taking it out of the darkness, is beautiful, but it is not easy. The usual thing is that it remains imprisoned.

One will not be able to enjoy authentic illumination as long as the essence, the consciousness, the soul, is bottled up, imprisoned. Behold the gravity of this matter...

Then it is necessary, perforce, to destroy, to disintegrate heroically, with a heroism superior to that of Napoleon in his great battles, or superior to that of Morelos in his fight for freedom, etc. It takes unparalleled heroism to free the poor soul, to get it out of the darkness. It is necessary first of all, as I said on the last occasion here to our brothers and sisters, to know well the techniques, the procedures that lead to the destruction of those "elements" where the soul is bottled up, imprisoned, so that enlightenment can come.

Observation: Directed Attention

First of all, we must begin by comprehending the need to know how to observe. We are, for example, sitting here, all of us, in these chairs; we know that we are sitting, but we have not *observed* these chairs.

In the first case, we have the knowledge that we are sitting on them, but observing them is already something else. In the first case, there is knowledge, but not observation. Observation requires a special concentration. Observe what they are made of, and then go into meditation, discover their atoms, their molecules... This already requires, let's say, directed attention...

Knowing that one is sitting in a chair is undirected attention, passive attention, but looking at the chair is directed attention.

Likewise, we can think a lot about ourselves, but this does not mean that we are observing our thoughts. Observing is different.

We live in a world of inferior emotions. Anything produces inferior emotions in us, and we know that we have them. But it is one thing to know that one is in a negative mood, and another thing to observe the negative mood, which is something completely different...

For example, on a certain occasion, a gentleman told a psychologist, "I feel antipathy for a certain person," and he quoted his name and surnames.

The psychologist replied, "Observe that person."

The interrogator answered again, he said, "But, how am I going to observe that person, when I know that person?"

The psychologist concluded that he did not want to observe, that he "knew," but did not *observe*. Knowing is one thing, and observing is quite another thing. One can know that one has a negative thought, but that does not mean that one is observing it. One knows that one is in a negative mood, but one has not observed that negative mood...

In practical life, we see that within us there are many things that should cause us shame: ridiculous comedies, inner questions, protests, morbid thoughts, etc.; but knowing that you have them is not the same as observing them.

Someone can say, "Yes, right now I have a morbid thought," but it is one thing to know that you have it and another thing is to observe it, which is totally different.

So, if one wants to get rid of this or that undesirable psychological element, first of all, one has to learn to observe with the purpose of changing, because, certainly, if one does not learn to self-observe, any possibility of change is impossible...

When one learns to self-observe, the sense of self-observation develops in oneself. Usually this sense is atrophied in the human race, it is degenerated, but as we use it, it unfolds and develops.

As a first point of view, we come to evidence through self-observation that even the most insignificant thoughts or the most ridiculous comedies that happen internally and that are never externalized, do not belong to our essence, they are created by others: by our "I's."

What is grave is to identify oneself with those comedies, with those ridiculous things, with those protests, with those angers, etc. If one identifies with any inferior extreme of these, the "I" that produces them becomes stronger, and thus, any possibility of elimination becomes more and more difficult. So, when it comes to bringing about a radical change in ourselves, observation is vital...

The different "I's" that live inside our psyche are very cunning, very sagacious; oftentimes they appeal to the "roll" of memories that we carry in the intellectual center...

Let us suppose that in the past one was fornicating with a person of the opposite sex, and that one is insisting, or not, in eliminating lust; then the ego of lust will appeal, it will

seize the center of memories of the intellectual center; that
"I" will grab there, let's say, the "roll" of memories, of scenes
of lubricity and he will pass them off as the person's fantasy,
and he will become more invigorated, he will become stronger
and stronger.

Because of all these things, you must see the need for
self-observation. Therefore, a radical and truly definitive
change would not be possible if we did not learn to observe
ourselves...

Knowing is not observing.

Thinking is not observing, either. Many believe that thinking of oneself is observing, but it is not. One can be thinking
of oneself, and yet one is not observing oneself. Thinking of
oneself is as different from observing as thirst is from water,
or as water from thirst!

The Observer and the Observed

Obviously, one must not identify with any of the "I's."

To observe oneself, one has to divide oneself into two: a
part that observes and another that is observed.

When the observing part sees the ridiculousness and non-
sense of the observed part, there is possibility of a change...

Let us take the example of discovering an "I" of anger...
When observing it, we can see that this "I" is not us, that he is
he. We could exclaim, "That 'I' has anger. I have no anger, but
that 'I' has it! Therefore it must die, I am going to work on it
to disintegrate it..." But if you identify with anger and say, "I
am angry, I am furious!" Anger becomes stronger, more and
more vigorous, and then how are you going to dissolve anger,
in what way? You couldn't, right? So, you shouldn't identify with that anger, or with his tantrum, or with his tragedy,
because if one becomes identified with its creation, well, one
ends up living in that creation as well, and that is absurd.

As one works on oneself, one goes deeper and deeper into
the issues of self-observation, one goes deeper and deeper. In
this, even the most insignificant thought must be observed.
Any desire, however transient it might be, any reaction, must

be reason for observation, because any desire, any reaction, any negative thought, comes from this or that "I."

And if we want to create light, liberate the soul, are we going to allow those "I's" to continue to exist? That would be absurd!

But, if what we want is light, if we are truly in love with light, we have to disintegrate the "I's." There is no other choice but to turn them into dust. We cannot turn to dust what we have not observed. Then, we need to know how to observe.

Internal Chatter vs. Silence of the Mind

In any case, we also have to take care of internal chatter, because there are many negative, absurd inner dialogues, inner conversations that never are exteriorized. Naturally, we need to correct that inner chatter, to learn to keep silent: "to know how to speak when one should speak, and to know how to keep silent when one should keep silent." This is the law not only for the physical world or the exterior world, but also for the interior world.

These negative inner chats, later externalize physically. That is why it is so important to eliminate inner negative chat, because it causes harm. You have to learn how to keep inner silence...

Usually "mental silence" is understood by emptying the mind of all kinds of thoughts, when one achieves stillness and silence of the mind through meditation, etc. But there is another kind of silence. Let us suppose that a case of critical judgment is presented to us in relation to a fellow man, and nevertheless, mentally we remain silent. We do not judge, we do not condemn. We are silent externally and internally. In this case, there is inner silence.

The facts of practical life, after all, must be kept in close correspondence with perfect inner conduct. When the facts of practical life agree with perfect inner conduct, it is a sign that we are already creating, in ourselves, the famous mental body.

If we put the different parts of a radio or tape recorder on a table, but we don't know anything about electronics, then we won't be able to capture the different "soundless" vibrations that swarm in the cosmos either; but if by comprehension we put the parts together, we will have the radio, we will have the device that can pick up sounds that we would not otherwise pick up. Likewise, the different parts of these studies, of this work, complement each other to form a wonderful body, the famous body of the mind. This body will allow us to better capture everything within ourselves, and will further develop the sense of intimate self-observation, and that is quite important.

Thus, the object of observation is to make a change within ourselves, to promote a true, effective change...

The Steps to Eliminate Defects

Once we have become skillful in self-observation, then the process of elimination becomes possible. There are three steps:

- First, observation

- Second, critical judgment

- Third, the elimination of a psychological "I"

When observing an "I," we must see:

- how it behaves in the intellectual center, and all its "games" with the mind

- second, how it is expressed through emotions in the heart

- third, its mode of action in the lower centers (motor, instinctive and sexual).

Obviously, in the sexual center, an "I" has one form of expression, in the heart it has another form, in the brain another. In the brain, an "I" manifests itself through the intellectual matters, namely reasons, justifications, evasions, loopholes, etc.; while in the heart it is a suffering, affection, what appears to be love but is really lust, etc.; and in the motor-instinctual-sexual centers, it has another form of expression as action, instinct, lascivious impulse, etc.

For example, let's cite a specific case: lust. Seeing a person of the opposite sex, an "I" of lust may manifest in the mind with constant thoughts. It could manifest itself in the heart as affection, as an apparently pure love, clean of all stains, to such an extent that one could perfectly justify oneself and say, "I do not feel lust for this person, what I am feeling is love..." But if one is observant, if one is very careful with one's own machine and observes the sexual center, one comes to discover that in the sexual center there is a certain activity related to that person. Then one proves that there is no affection or love, but lust. Behold how delicate the crime is: lust can perfectly disguise itself in the heart as love, compose verses, etc., etc., but it is disguised lust...

If one is careful and observes those three centers of the human machine, one can see that it is an "I," and discovered that it is an "I," having known its behavior in the three centers (intellect, heart, and sex), then one proceeds to the third phase.

What is the third phase? It is execution! It is the final phase of the work: execution! Then one has to appeal to prayer in the work. What is meant by "prayer in the work"? Prayer in the work must be done on the basis of intimate self-remembering...

Four States of Consciousness

There are four states of consciousness.[4]

The first state of consciousness is that of the deep and unconscious sleep of a person, of an ego that left the body asleep in bed, but wanders in the molecular world in a "coma state" (it is the lowest state).

The second state of consciousness is that of the dreamer who has returned to the physical body, and who believes

---

4   In yoga: deep sleep (sushupti), dreaming (svapna), waking (jagrat), and superconscious (turiya). In Greek, these are eikasia, pistis, dianoia, and nous. Read *The Perfect Matrimony* by Samael Aun Weor.

that one is awake; the person is still dreaming but with the physical body in a waking state. This second type of dreamer is more dangerous, because they can kill, they can steal, they can commit crimes of all kinds. In the first case, the dreamer is more subhuman and cannot do any of these things. How could it, how could it hurt someone? When the body is passive and dreaming, the person cannot harm anyone in the physical world. But when the body is active and still dreaming, the person can do a lot of damage in the physical world. That is why the sacred scriptures insist on the need to wake up.

These two types of people are in a state of profound unconsciousness, and continue to dream; if they pray, those two infrahuman states create only negative results, because nature responds... For example, an unconscious person, asleep, prays to start a business, but his "I's," which are so innumerable, do not agree with what he is doing, because only one of the "I's" is making the prayer; the others have not been taken into account; those others may not be interested in that business, they do not agree with that prayer, and thus, they ask for the exact opposite in the prayer so that that business fails; since the opposed are majority, nature answers with an influx of forces and the business fails, that is clear.

So, for prayer to be effective in working on oneself, one has to place oneself in the third state of consciousness, which is intimate remembrance of oneself, the remembrance of one's Being...[5]

Immersed in deep meditation, concentrated on one's inner Divine Mother, beg her to eliminate from one's psyche, to separate and eliminate from one's psyche that "I" that one wants to disintegrate.

It may be that the Divine Mother at that moment acts, decapitating that ego, but that does not mean the work is

---

5 A state of active consciousness, controlled by will, that begins with awareness of being here and now. This state has many levels (see: Consciousness). True Self-remembering occurs without thought or mental processing: it is a state of conscious perception and includes the remembrance or awareness of the inner Being. Read *Light from Darkness* by Samael Aun Weor.

done. The Divine Mother is not going to instantly disintegrate all of it.

If the whole of it is not disintegrated, one needs to have patience. In successive works, over time, that "I" slowly disintegrates, losing its volume, size...

An "I" can be frighteningly horrible, but as it loses volume it becomes more beautiful; it takes the appearance of a child, and finally it turns to dust. When it has turned to dust, the consciousness that was inserted, bottled up, stuffed inside that "I," is released. Then the light will have increased. A percentage of light is free. This is how we will proceed with each of the "I's.".

The work is long and very hard. Often times a negative thought, no matter how insignificant it may be, is based on an ancient "I." A negative thought that comes to mind indicates that there is an "I" behind that thought, and that this "I" must be removed, eradicated from our psyche.

You have to study it, get to know its conduct, and see how it behaves in the three centers: in the intellectual, in the emotional (and speaking in synthesis), in the motor-instinctual-sexual. See how it works in each of the three centers. According to its behavior, one gets to know each "I.".

When one has developed the sense of self-observation, one comes to prove for oneself that some of those "I's" are terrifyingly horrible, they are true monsters, horrifying, macabre figures who live in our psyche. They live in our psyche because some sacred individuals made a mistake and implanted the abominable Kundabuffer organ in the nature of the human being.

Now, how can we stop being monsters?

Kundalini

It is necessary to implant in the human organism another organ like that of the Kundabuffer, but one that is positive, luminous, antithetical, opposite to the Kundabuffer. It exists, and it is the Kundalini. The word "kunda" reminds us of the abominable Kundabuffer organ. "Lini" means termination, the termination of the abominable Kundabuffer organ. That is, as the Kundalini serpent ascends, the abominable Kundabuffer organ is reduced to cosmic dust.

In Genesis, the Kundabuffer organ appears as the tempting serpent of Eden, and is the horrible Python with seven heads, which crawled through the mud of the earth, and which irritated Apollo wounded with his darts; it is the same abominable Kundabuffer organ.

In ancient wisdom, the Kundalini appears to Moses as the serpent of bronze, as the Kundalini coiled around the Tao or generating lingam.

> *"And the people spoke (better said: blasphemed: fornicated)[6] against Elohim, and against Moses (the Son of Man), Wherefore have ye brought us up (into Tiphereth - Eloah Va Daath Iod-Havah - יהוה אלוה ודעת) out of Mitzrayim (מצרים Malkuth) to die (psychologically) in the wilderness (במדבר Bamidbar - the mind)? for there is no bread, neither is there any water; and (נפש Nephesh) our (animal) soul detest this light bread (better said: the animal soul detest the bread of light).*

> *"And (because of the animal orgasm of the animal soul) Iod-Havah (יהוה) sent (kundabuffers or) burning serpents (of lust הנחשים השרפים) among the people, and they bit the people; and many people (archetypes) of Israel died (in Tiphereth).*

> *"Therefore, the people came to Moses, and said, We have sinned, for we have spoken against Iod-Havah (the Holy Spirit), and against thee (the Son of man); pray unto Iod-Havah, that he take away the (lustful kundabuffer) serpents from us.*

---

6   "Wherefore I say unto you, All manner of sin and blasphemy shall be forgiven unto men: but the blasphemy against (Binah, Iod-Hava Elohim) the Holy Spirit (that is fornication) shall not be forgiven unto men. And whosoever speaketh a word against the Son of man, it shall be forgiven him: but whosoever speaks against the Holy Spirit, it shall not be forgiven him, neither in this world, neither in the world to come." — Matthew 12:31-32

Kundalini and Kundabuffer in the Bible

"And Moses prayed for the people. And Iod-Havah said unto Moses, Make thee a (שרף Seraph or kundalini) fiery serpent (of chastity), and set it upon a pole (the spinal medulla): and it shall come to pass, that every one that is bitten, when he looks upon it, shall live.

"And Moses made (that is, the people by means of willpower rose the kundalini or) a serpent of brass, and put it upon a pole (their spinal medulla), and it came to pass, that if any (נחש נחשת nahash nahashoth) serpent (kundabuffer) had bitten any male fire (איש), when beholding (for protection) the (kundalini or) serpent of brass, they lived." —Numbers 21: 5-9

Gurdjieff made the mistake of confusing the Kundalini with the Kundabuffer, the serpent that goes up with the serpent that goes down. Gurdjieff attributed to the serpent that goes up all the sinister tenebrous powers of the descending serpent; that's where his mistake was.[7] This is the reason why Gurdjieff's disciples were unable to dissolve the "I's." That was his big mistake.

On the basis of mere comprehension it is not possible to dissolve the "I's." I do not deny that with the knife of the consciousness, vividly comprehending any "I," we can separate it from ourselves, from our psyche; but that is not enough. Any "I" separated from our psyche will continue to live. It will not resign itself to staying away from home; it will try again and again to take its place within us; it will become a tempting demon.

We have to disintegrate the "I" we have separated from ourselves with the knife of the consciousness. No one can disintegrate them with a power other than the power of the Divine Mother Kundalini. Only she can reduce it to ashes, to cosmic dust.

Thus, the fundamental thing, my dear brothers and sisters, is to die in oneself, definitively, in order to open the inner mind, and enjoy objective reasoning, which is true cognition of reality, intimate experience of the Being, transcendental,

---

7   Similarly, today people who believe they are awakening Kundalini with their fornication are actually developing the Kundabuffer.

divine, buddhic vision, beyond the body, the affections, and the subjective mind.

As you digest all this, you will also understand the need to live alert and vigilant like a sentinel in times of war, always working constantly.

The way you are right now, you are useless.[8]

You have a wrong creation within, manifesting through a false personality.

Spiritually you are dead. You have no reality.

You must cease to be as you are now, because if you continue to exist as you are, you will have to enter the mineral devolution within the bowels of the Earth.[9]

As you are now, you are spiritually dead. You do not possess the objective reasoning of the Being. You have not achieved enlightenment. You are like shadows within the deep darknesses.

What is your reality? Shadows, and nothing more than that: shadows.

You need to open your inner mind,[10] and for this you have to cease to exist like miserable shadows.

You have to become merciless with yourselves. Today you love yourselves very much, you consider yourself too much. But what do you love? Your dear ego, your nakedness, your

---

8   "We have to situate ourselves in the plane of the crudest realities. In no way have I come here with the purpose of being pessimistic, nor do I intend to fill your hearts with pessimism: I have only wanted to put on the table of realities, the psychological state in which each and every one of us find ourselves. As long as we have not eliminated from our interior all those selves-defects that we carry, our consciousness will be profoundly asleep; we will die without knowing what time; we will be born without knowing how or why; we will continue in the afterlife like somnambulists, like ghosts. This has been our life. So, our life has been and so it will be, as long as we do not eliminate the ego-defects from our interior." —Samael Aun Weor, the lecture "The Meaning of Life, the Two Lines of Life, and Our Level of Being"

9   Read *Hell, the Devil, and Karma* by Samael Aun Weor.

10 "One who has opened the inner mind recalls one's previous existences, knows the mysteries of life and death; not because of what one has or has not read, not because of what someone has or has not said, not because of what one has or has not believed, but because of terribly real and vivid direct experience." —Samael Aun Weor, *The Great Rebellion*

inner misery, the darkness within which you find yourselves? Is that what you love so much?

Stop, brothers and sisters!

Reflect deeply.

Reflect.

You must dedicate yourselves to working intensely on yourselves.

You must comprehend the process of lust, which is the worst enemy of the elimination, the worst enemy of the dissolution of your ego.

Who does not have ego? Who has not had ego? It must be reduced to ashes.

Does any brother or sister have something to ask? Speak, sister.

STUDENT: Venerable, Gurdjieff is called master. Did he work in the ninth sphere, or did he only work on the dissolution of the ego?

SAMAEL AUN WEOR: Gurdjieff worked in the ninth sphere, he manufactured the superior existential bodies of the Being, but he did not achieve the total dissolution of his ego because he rejected his Divine Mother. How can the ungrateful child dissolve the ego? The ungrateful child does not progress in these studies. First of all, before we get to the Father, we have to get to the Mother, that's obvious!

Does any other brother or sister have something to ask regarding this?

STUDENT: Master, since Gurdjieff was your disciple, how did he not know that the only path for the dissolution of the ego was with the Divine Mother Kundalini?

SAMAEL AUN WEOR: Gurdjieff forgot about his Mother. In former existences he was under my instruction, but in his last existence, since he was far from me, he also forgot about his Divine Mother. That was his mistake, that! Without that fohatic power, no one can disintegrate the psychic aggregates. By themselves, they will not achieve anything. The knife of the consciousness allows one to separate the "I's" that one has comprehended, in order to separate them from one's psyche, but that does not mean dissolution. I repeat, such "I's" will fight incessantly to return to accommodate themselves within the organic machine.

Is there any other brother or sister who has something to ask? I do not want you not to ask, but to ask; because if one does not ask, one has not comprehended. There are times when you need to ask. Parsifal in his first arrival at the castle of Montsalvat, of the transcendent Monsalvat, did not become King of the Grail because of not having asked the reason for the pains of Amfortas. So you always have to ask... Speak up, brother.

STUDENT: Master, how many processes are required to acquire the objective reasoning of the Being?

SAMAEL Aun Weor: In order to attain objective reasoning there are six degrees. Obviously, objective reasoning has six degrees, but the highest of the six degrees belongs to the sacred Anklad, and this is three steps away from the infinitude that sustains all.

Did you ask how many processes are required? You have to first die completely within yourself.[11] If you do not disintegrate the ego, you do not develop objective reasoning. But as you advance deeply in the destruction of the myself, the objective reasoning of the Being opens up.

Thus, when you achieve one hundred percent of dissolution of the ego, the objective reasoning of the Being in yourself will have reached the fullness of perfection; then you will be enlightened, absolutely enlightened, and you will know through lived, direct experience all the mysteries of the universe. You will not ignore anything, and you will have all the powers of the cosmos. This is beyond the chakras. Listen, the chakras are but dim lights compared to the sunlight of objective reasoning.

---

11 I.e. all defects must be eliminated.

The Mysteries of the Fire

In the Vestibule of Wisdom

Beloved disciple,

Many books have been written about Oriental yoga. Yoga योग means "union with God." All the books that were written about Oriental yoga before now are antiquated for the new era of Aquarius, which began the fourth of February 1962, between the hours of two and three in the afternoon.

This book entitled *Kundalini Yoga* is for the new Aquarian era. Through this book we teach our disciples a practical religion. All religions teach unbreakable dogmas we are supposed to believe, even when their truths cannot be seen with eyes of the flesh. Regarding the former statement, we, the Gnostics, are a little different. We teach the human being to see, hear, touch, and perceive all of the divine mysteries, the ineffable things, etc. from beyond the grave.

We sustain that human beings have a sixth sense, and that through this sixth sense they can see the angels and converse with them.

We asseverate that human beings have a seventh sense called "intuition." Thus, when human beings awaken that seventh sense they can know the great mysteries of life and death. Then, they do not need to study these mysteries in any book. So, beloved reader, this book is for that purpose.

You will find terrific secrets within this book, secrets that before now were never published in the history of life.

We respect all religions profoundly. Not only do we respect them, but moreover, we teach our disciples how to see, hear, touch, and perceive the essential truths that all religions teach in their sacred books.

Therefore, this book that you have in your hands is a book of terrific secrets that have never been published before. You can develop your hidden powers to see, hear, touch and perceive the Angels, Archangels, Seraphim, Powers, Virtues, etc. With this book you can attain yoga, union with God.

The Holy Bible discloses great truths; thus, we read within the Bible how the prophets of God had the power to

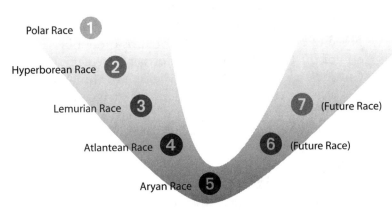

Polar Race ①

Hyperborean Race ②

Lemurian Race ③

⑦ (Future Race)

Atlantean Race ④

⑥ (Future Race)

Aryan Race ⑤

Seven Root Races

talk with the angels. This book that you have in your hands belongs to the Gnostic Christian Universal Church; read it, study it, and meditate on it. This is the yoga of the new era of Aquarius.

You will find a glossary at the end of this book with the explanation of the meaning of many words that you may not know. Therefore, search in the glossary for the meaning of each word that you do not know.

We are entering the ethereal world, where the human being has to conquer the fifth element of nature, the ether. The ethereal world [fourth dimension] has to be the conquest of the Aryan race.[1] Gross materialism must fall wounded before the majesty of the ether. This book is for those who indeed want to transform themselves into angels.

Every planet gives birth to seven root races; thereafter it dies. Our planet Earth already gave birth to five root races; two more root races are needed.

There are seven elements[2] of nature.

The first root race lived in the polar cap of the north and conquered the fire.

The second root race, after having fought against the tempestuous atmosphere of the air from the second continent, the Hyperborean continent, finally attained the conquest of the air and adapted themselves to its environment.

The third root race lived in Lemuria, fighting against the tempestuous seas, and was removed by incessant seaquakes. The third root race conquered the water.

The fourth root race lived in the continent of Atlantis within an aqueous atmosphere. Human beings breathed though gills; but a total transformation happened in the human physiognomy with the Deluge:[3] the human being developed lungs and adapted to the new atmosphere. Then the human being perceived the physical world with sight, and conquered the element earth.

---

1 The term Aryan refers to most people, not one group. Read "Aryan Race" in the glossary.
2 Also called tattvas, "fundamental principles," the essential nature of a given thing.
3 The Universal Flood known in all ancient traditions.

Presently we are in the Aryan root race, which populates the five continents of the world. The triumph of this root race has not yet been achieved. The Aryan root race will conquer the ether. Atomic investigations will take the human being to the conquest of ether.

Interplanetary ships occupied by people from other worlds, from different planets of the solar system, will come to the Earth. These types of ships are owned by any advanced humanity from any of the planets of space. However, these cosmic ships have not been delivered to this terrestrial humanity for the simple fact that they will use them in order to perpetrate in other planets the same barbarian invasions that they accomplished here in their historical conquests. The people from any of the planets of this solar system are already very advanced and they know very well the state of barbarism in which we, the inhabitants of Earth, are found. Nevertheless, in the new era of Aquarius, the inhabitants of the different worlds of the solar system will establish official contact with our planet Earth. Human beings from other humanities—like Venus, Mars, Mercury, etc.—will come in interplanetary ships, and many people will go aboard those ships to visit the planets of the solar system. Those advanced humanities will teach the human being how to build interplanetary ships. This is how "official" science will be fulminated, and human pride will be wounded to death by the advanced humanities from this solar system.[4]

In the new Aquarian era, the Aryan root race will conquer the interplanetary ether, and cosmic trips to other planets will become routine. Cultural and commercial interaction will be established with all of the solar system; thus, as a consequence, the human being will elevate to a high cultural level.[5]

Later on, the sixth root race that will inhabit the continent of Antarctica will conquer the Astral Light.

The seventh root race will conquer the cosmic mind; then, the human being will elevate to the angelic kingdom.

---

4   Read *Cosmic Ships* by Samael Aun Weor.
5

Nonetheless, I tell you, beloved reader, that with this book that you have in your hands, right now, you can transform into a terrific divine angel, if that is what you want. What is important is for you to practice the terrific divine science which we are delivering to you in this book.

May peace be with all of humanity.

Mantra Pronunciation

There are some sacred words (mantras) taught in this book. Generally speaking, the sounds in mantras are pronounced using the ancient roots (Latin, Sanskrit, etc):

I: as the ee in "tree"

E: as the eh in "they"

O: as the oh in "holy"

U: as the u in "true"

A: as the ah in "father"

M: extended as if humming, "mmmmm"

S: extended like a hiss, "sssss"

G: In most mantras, G is pronounced as in "give"

Vajrayogini

Tibetan Buddhist symbol of the Divine Mother as the destroyer
of the causes of suffering. Note her spear, knife, and cup, and the
necklace of skulls that represent the defects she has destroyed.

Chapter 1

The Universal Fire

1. Maha-Kundalini[1] is Fohat.[2]

2. Maha-Kundalini is the universal fire of life.

3. The universal fire has seven degrees of power.

4. Oh Devi Kundalini! You are the fire of the seven Laya centers[3] of the universe.

5. The seven Laya centers of the universe are the seven degrees of power of the fire.

6. There are seven churches in the Chaos[4] where the seven planetary Logoi[5] officiate.

7. These seven churches are also within the spinal medulla of the human being.

8. The seven planetary Logoi officiated in their seven temples in the dawn of life.

9. The seven saints practiced the rituals of Maha-Kundalini within the sacred precinct of their temples in the dawn of the mahamanvantara.[6]

10. The material universe did not exist.

11. The universe solely existed within the mind of the gods.

12. Nonetheless, for the gods, the universe was ideal and objective, simultaneously.

13. The universe was; yet, it did not exist.

14. The universe "is;" yet, it does not exist within the bosom of the Absolute.

15. To **be** is better than to exist.

---

1 Sanskrit महाकुण्डलिनी, "great fire," the Divine Mother.
2 Cosmic fire. See glossary.
3 A cosmic point where matter disappears from one dimension and passes to exist in another dimension. See glossary.
4 Greek χάος khaos, the primitive state of the universe, from which occurs creation (Genesis).
5 Greek, "words," manifested deities.
6 Sanskrit, "great cosmic time of activity."

The Seven Serpents of Kundalini

16. The seven saints fecundated the chaotic matter so that universal life could emerge.

17. Devi Kundalini has seven degrees of power.

18. There are seven serpents: two groups of three, plus the sublime coronation of the seventh tongue of fire that unites us with the One, with the Law, with the Father.

19. These seven degrees of power of the fire differentiated the chaotic matter in seven states of matter upon which the perceptions of our seven senses are based.

20. The seven igneous serpents of each of the planetary Logoi fecundated the chaotic matter so that life could emerge.

21. Before the dawn of the aurora of the mahamanvantara, Sattva, Rajas, and Tamas[7] were in a perfect, Nirvanic equilibrium.

22. Fire put the cosmic scale in motion.

23. Sattva, Rajas, and Tamas became unbalanced; thus, this is how the mahamanvantara dawned.

24. In order to gain the right to enter into the Absolute, the yogi/yogini must liberate the Self from Sattva, Rajas, and Tamas.

25. At the end of the mahamanvantara, Sattva, Rajas, and Tamas will again be in perfect equilibrium; thus, the universe will sleep again within the profound bosom of the Absolute, within the supreme Parabrahman,[8] the Nameless.

26. The universe will sleep for seven eternities, until Maha-Kundalini awakens it again to activity.

27. The Chaos is the raw matter of the Great Work.

28. The Chaos is the Mulaprakriti,[9] the primordial matter.

29. Mulaprakriti is Christonic semen,[10] from which the universe emerged.

30. We have Mulaprakriti in our sexual organs, and thence it springs up life.

31. Upon the altars of the temples of the seven planetary Logoi we see seven sacred vessels filled with Christonic semen.

32. That is the sacred symbol of Mulaprakriti.

33. Those are the primordial waters of life.

34. The water is the habitat of fire.

---

7   The three gunas that symbolize the fundamental principles of existence. See glossary "gunas."

8   Sanskrit, "beyond the creator god."

9   (Sanskrit मूलप्रकृति) Literally, the "root or origin of nature; primary cause; original root or germ out of which matter or all apparent forms are evolved." The abstract feminine principle. Undifferentiated substance.

10 Latin, "seed," the sexual power, whether in males or females.

The Divine Mother as fire and coiled serpent

35. The one who wastes the water also wastes the fire and remains in darkness.

36. The seven saints fecundated the Christonic semen of the universe so that life could sprout.

37. The yogi/yogini has to fecundate one's primordial waters, one's Christonic semen, with the grandiose power of Devi Kundalini.

38. Kundalini is the spouse of Shiva,[11] the Innermost, the Purusha.[12]

39. Kundalini is the spirit of electricity.

40. Electricity is the sexual power of Maha-Kundalini.

41. Kundalini is coiled within the chakra Muladhara.[13]

42. Kundalini is the serpent whose tail is coiled three and a half times.

43. When Kundalini awakens, it hisses as the serpents hisses.

---

11 The Hindu symbol of the third aspect of the trinity / trimurti (Brahma, Vishnu, Shiva). The Third Logos. The Holy Spirit. The Sexual Force. The Sephirah Binah.

12 Sanskrit पुरुष "supreme self or being."

13 An energetic center at the base of the spine.

44. Prana,[14] buddhi,[15] indriyas,[16] ahamkara,[17] mind, the seven elements of nature, nerves, are in their totality products of Kundalini.

45. Kundalini is intimately related with the prana that circulates throughout the 72,000 nadis,[18] astral conduits that nourish the chakras.

46. The chakras are connected with the mind.

47. Yogi and yogini have to christify their mind.

48. Prana is life, and it circulates throughout all of our organs.

49. Prana circulates throughout all of our nadis and vital canals.

50. All of the 72,000 nadis of our organism have their fundamental base in the nadi kanda.[19]

51. The nadi kanda is situated between the sexual organs and the anus.

---

14 Life force.

15 Intellect.

16 Senses.

17 The feeling of individuality.

18 Sanskrit नदी, river, conduit, artery. Subtle channels for energy. In Asian mysticism, large numbers like "72,000" are not meant to be taken literally. "The term Nadi comes from the root Nad which means motion. The body is filled with an uncountable number of Nadis. If they were revealed to the eye, the body would present the appearance of a highly-complicated chart of ocean currents. Superficially the water seems one and the same. But examination shows that it is moving with varying degrees of force in all directions." —Swami Sivananda

19 "This is situated between the anus and the root of the reproductory organ. It is like the shape of an egg and is covered with membranes. This is just above the Muladhara Chakra. All the Nadis of the body spring from this Kanda. It is in the junction where Sushumna is connected with Muladhara Chakra. The four petals of the Muladhara Chakra are on the sides of this Kanda and the junction is called Granthi-Sthana, where the influence of Maya is very strong. In some Upanishads you will find that Kanda is 9 digits above the genitals. Kanda is a centre of the astral body from where Yoga Nadis, subtle channels, spring and carry the Sukshma Prana (vital energy) to the different parts of the body." - Swami Sivananda, Kundalini Yoga

52. The kanda collects all of the sexual energy that circulates throughout the 72,000 canals of our organism.

53. The sexual energy is prana, life.

54. The Angel Aroch (angel of power) taught us the pranava[20] **Kandil, Bandil, R** for the awakening of Devi Kundalini.

55. These mantras act on the kanda, reinforcing the vibration of prana.

56. Thus, the spouse of Shiva, who is coiled in the chakra Muladhara, is awakened when prana is reinforced.

57. The correctly chanted pronunciation of this pranava is as follows:

58. *KAN dil... BAN dil... Rrrrrrrrrrr...*

59. KAN is pronounced aloud. DIL is pronounced with a low voice.

60. BAN is pronounced aloud. DIL is pronounced with a low voice.

61. The letter R has to be rolled and acutely pronounced, imitating the sound produced by the rattles of the rattlesnake.

62. This is how the prana is reinforced, so that from the kanda—where the Sushumna nadi[21] and the chakra Muladhara are joined—Devi Kundalini awakens.

63. The kanda is precisely situated in the same point where the nadi Sushumna and the chakra Muladhara join.

64. This is why the pranava of the Angel Aroch acts so intensely on the Kundalini.

65. The kanda nourishes itself with the sexual organs.

66. The kanda has its physiological correspondence in the "cauda equina" of the spinal medulla.

67. The spinal medulla begins in the spinal bulbar region (this refers to the medulla oblongata, which looks like a swelling, or bulb, at the top of the spinal cord), and ends in the cauda equina (because of their appearance,

---

20 Sanskrit "sacred word," also called mantra.
21 The subtle (sukshma) central conduit in the spinal column.

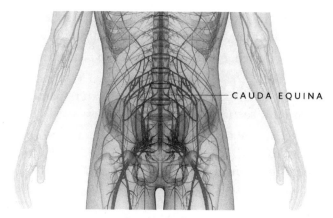

Cauda Equina

the obliquely coursing fine nerve roots or nerve fibers are named the cauda equina, a Latin term for "horse's tail"), that form the inferior extreme of the spinal medulla.

68. Prana is sexual.

69. Sexual energy is solar.

70. Solar energy is Christic.[22]

71. Prana is Christic.

72. The Cosmic Christ is the Solar Logos.

73. Solar energy comes from the Cosmic Christ.

74. Christic prana makes the spike of wheat grow; thus, the Christic substance—ready to be devoured—remains enclosed within the grain.

75. Water from the mountain glaciers penetrates within the stump to ripen the grape, within which the whole life, the whole prana from the Sun-Christ, remains enclosed.

76. This is why the bread and the wine[23] symbolize the flesh and blood of the martyr of Calvary.

77. All vegetables evolve with the potent force of the Solar Logos.

---

22 The Cosmic Christ is a force, as electricity or gravity are. See glossary.

23 The blessed food and drink of the Christian ritual, equivalent to prasad, kiddush, ganapuja / tsog / tsok, etc.

78. All food disarranges itself into billions of solar corpuscular energies within our organic laboratory.

79. People of science call these solar corpuscular energies "vitamins."

80. The best of the radiant force of the Sun remains enclosed within our sexual glands.

81. The very aroma of the Sun, the most powerful solar atoms, form that semi-solid, semi-liquid substance that is called Christonic semen or Mulaprakriti.

82. Mulaprakriti is the Cosmic Christ in substance.

83. Therefore, the entire power of Devi Kundalini is within our Christonic semen.

84. Whosoever wants to awaken Devi Kundalini has to be absolutely chaste.[24]

85. Whosoever wants to awaken Devi Kundalini has to know how to wisely control the sexual forces.

86. The wise control of the sexual energies is called Sexual Magic.

87. No yogi/yogini can totally Christify the Self without Sexual Magic.

88. The kanda is situated within the chakra Muladhara.

89. The chakra Muladhara has four resplendent petals.

90. The kanda has the shape of an egg.

91. The kanda nourishes itself with the Cosmic Christ.

92. When the Kundalini awakens, it rises throughout the spinal medulla.

93. The Brahmanadi[25] or "canalis centralis"[26] within which the Kundalini ascends is throughout the length of the spinal medulla.

---

24 Sexually pure, not abstinent. See glossary.

25 Sanskrit ब्राह्मणादि "channel of Brahma" from ब्रह्मन् Brahma, the highest form of divinity, and nadī नदी, "river, conduit, artery." A subtle conduit in the center of the spinal column, through which energy can flow. In most people, it is dormant.

26 The cerebrospinal fluid-filled space that runs through the spinal cord.

94. Our planet Earth also has a spinal column.

95. The spinal column of our planet Earth is Mount Meru, situated in the Himalayas.

96. The chakra Muladhara is the abode of Devi Kundalini.

97. The chakra Muladhara is situated at the very root of our sexual organs.

98. Therefore, the chakra Muladhara is totally sexual and can be opened only with Sexual Magic.

99. Sexual Magic has always been taught in secrecy within the secret schools of Oriental yoga.

100. In our next chapters, we will teach to our disciples the complete Sexual Magic of India and Tibet, just as it has always been taught in the secret schools.

101. Now, it is necessary for our disciples to chant daily the pranava of the Angel Aroch.

102. It is urgent to vocalize daily these mantras for one hour.

103. This is how we will reinforce the prana, by intensely acting on the kanda, to awaken the spouse of Shiva, Devi Kundalini.

104. Maha-Kundalini underlies all organic and inorganic matter and is the cause of light, heat, electricity, and life.

105. In the this course of Kundalini Yoga, we will teach our disciples all of the secret science of Maha-Kundalini so that they can awaken all of their hidden powers and convert themselves into Logoi, into Dhyan-Choans, into Buddhas of Christic nature.

106. The pranava Kandil Bandil R must be sung by the male-female couple during Maithuna.

107. At the dawn of the mahamanvantara, the man was on the right and the woman on the left.

108. While seated, male and female chanted the sacred pranava of Maha-Kundalini.

109. At the dawn of the mahamanvantara, the seven planetary Logoi officiated the rituals of Maha-Kundalini in their temples.

110. I, Samael Aun Weor, was a witness of the dawn of the mahamanvantara.

111. I still remember when I was visiting the sacred temples of the Chaos.

112. In every temple there was an ineffable lady next to every Logos.

113. Indeed, the separated sexes did not exist, but the ineffable gods knew how to polarize themselves in accordance with the necessities of the moment.

114. The Elohim[27] or Prajapatis[28] are hermaphrodites.[29]

115. A Prajapati or Elohim can draw forth their masculine or feminine polarity; they know how to polarize themselves.

116. This is how the seven planetary Logoi could draw forth their masculine aspect.

117. This is how their Isis[30] could draw forth their feminine aspect.

118. Now our disciples will understand how inside each one of the temples of the Chaos the gods worked as couples, chanting the rhythms of fire.

119. Groups of children (Prajapatis or Elohim) formed choirs with these ineffable couples.

120. The sacred fire emerges from the brain of the Father and from the bosom of the Mother.

121. This coenobium of the sacred fire fecundated Mulaprakriti so that life could emerge.

122. The raw matter of the Great Work is the Christonic semen.

---

27 Hebrew, a plural word that simultaneously means a single god-goddess and multiple gods and goddesses. See glossary.
28 Sanskrit "Lords of Procreation"
29 A being capable of proliferating its species without sexual intercourse. See glossary.
30 Egyptian name for the Divine Mother.

123. The raw matter of the Great Work is the mazar of the gods, the sea of milk, the fountain of milk and of the coagulations, the water of Amrita.[31]

124. That is the sacred cow from where life emerges.

125. These are the primordial waters that are deposited within our sexual glands.

126. The Verb of the gods fecundated the chaotic matter so that life could emerge.

127. The throat is a uterus where the Word is gestated.

128. The throat is the sexual organ of the gods.

129. The Sexual Magic of the Word fecundated the chaotic matter so that life could emerge.

130. The creation of the universe was the outcome of the Sexual Magic of the Word.

131. The universe was elaborated with the Anu atom[32] within the profound bosom of Parabrahman.

132. The Anu atom cannot be multiplied or divided in the pro-genital or primogenital state.

133. All the atoms of the universe are nothing but passing vestures of the primordial Anu atom.

134. This primordial Anu atom is Nirvanic.

135. The objective material universe is born from a Nirvanic condensation.

136. The entire universe is granulated Fohat.

137. The entire material universe is elaborated with the granulations of Fohat.

---

31 The substance that gives immortality to the gods. Also called soma, ambrosia, nectar, etc.

32 "Anu is the primordial chaos, the god time and world at once, χρομος and Κοσμος, the uncreated matter issued from the one and fundamental principle of all things." - H.P. Blavatsky, Isis Unveiled

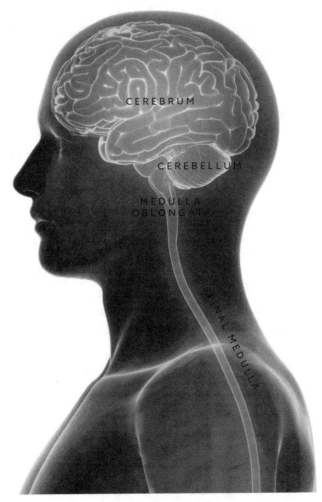

CEREBRUM

CEREBELLUM

MEDULLA
OBLONGATA

SPINAL MEDULLA

Cerebrospinal Nervous System

Chapter 2

The Degrees of Power of the Fire

1. The cerebrospinal nervous system is formed by: cerebrum, cerebellum, medulla oblongata, and spinal medulla.

2. The medulla oblongata connects the cerebellum with the sacred spinal medulla.

3. The medulla oblongata is intimately related with all of the so-called "involuntary functions" of our organic system.

4. The medulla begins on the top of the spinal canal and ends in the first vertebra of the coccygeal region.

5. The spinal medulla is a cord of gray and white material.

6. The gray matter is in the center of the spinal medulla and the white matter in its periphery.

7. The gray matter is formed in its conjunction by innumerable nervous cells and a multitude of nervous fibers.

8. The white matter is formed by nervous medullar matter.

9. All of this matter looks as if it is suspended from the medullar canal.

10. The nourishment of this fine medullar matter is performed by means of the delicate web of membranes that are around it.

11. The medulla and the brain are surrounded by a powerful liquid[33] mentioned by Mr. Leadbeater in one of his books.

12. This marvelous fluid protects the medulla and the brain.

13. The medulla is totally protected by a marvelous covering of innumerable fatty tissues.

---

33 Cerebrospinal fluid (CSF), clear, colourless liquid that fills and surrounds the brain and the spinal cord.

Seven Primary Chakras on the Spinal Column

14. The medulla is divided into two symmetrical parts, which are completely demarcated by two caesuras: the Sylvian fissure and the Rolandic fissure.

15. The "canalis centralis" exists throughout the length of the medulla.

16. The Brahmanadi runs throughout the length of this medullar canal from the chakra Muladhara[34] until the chakra Sahasrara.[35]

17. The Kundalini rises throughout this nadi until the Brahmarandhra.[36]

18. The Brahmarandhra is septuple in its internal constitution.

19. Each one of our seven bodies has its own spinal medulla and its Brahmanadi.

20. The Kundalini is constituted by seven serpents.

21. These seven serpents are the seven radicals.

22. These seven serpents of Devi Kundalini are the seven siblings of Fohat. These seven serpents of Devi Kundalini are the seven degrees of power of the fire.

23. The septenary constitution of the human being is:

    1. Atman: the innermost

    2. Buddhi: the consciousness, the divine soul

    3. Superior manas: the human soul, willpower, causal body

    4. Inferior manas: the mind, mental body

    5. Kama-rupa: the body of desires, the astral body

    6. Linga-sarira: the vital (ethereal) body

    7. Sthula-sarira: the physical body

24. Each one of these seven bodies has its own spinal medulla, its Sushumna-nadi, and its Brahmanadi.

---

34 At the base of the spine, and related to the sexual organs.

35 At the crown of the head.

36 "The hollow place in the crown of the head known as anterior fontanelle in the new-born child is the Brahmarandhra." —Swami Sivananda, Kundalini Yoga

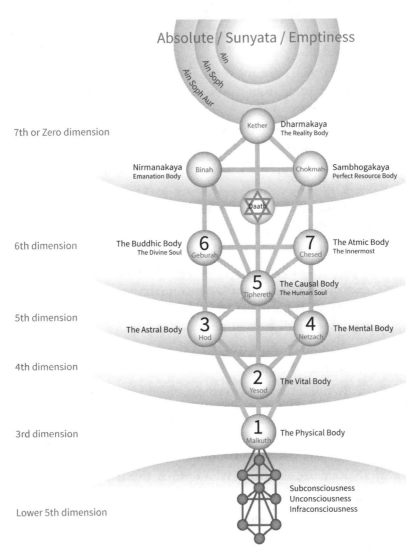

Absolute / Sunyata / Emptiness

Ain
Ain Soph
Ain Soph Aur

7th or Zero dimension

Kether — Dharmakaya
The Reality Body

Nirmanakaya — Binah
Emanation Body

Chokmah — Sambhogakaya
Perfect Resource Body

Daath

6th dimension

The Buddhic Body — 6 Geburah
The Divine Soul

7 Chesed — The Atmic Body
The Innermost

5 Tiphereth — The Causal Body
The Human Soul

5th dimension

The Astral Body — 3 Hod

4 Netzach — The Mental Body

4th dimension

2 Yesod — The Vital Body

3rd dimension

1 Malkuth — The Physical Body

Lower 5th dimension

Subconsciousness
Unconsciousness
Infraconsciousness

Seven Bodies on the Tree of Life (Kabbalah)

25. Seven are the serpents: two groups of three with the coronation of the seventh tongue of fire that unites us with the One, with the Law, with the Father.

26. These are the seven levels of knowledge.

27. These are the seven doorways of the seven great Initiations of Major Mysteries.[37]

28. Only the terror of love and law reign throughout these seven doorways.

29. The human being raises the first serpent through the first Initiation of Major Mysteries.

30. The human being raises the second serpent through the second Initiation of Major Mysteries, and likewise successively.

31. The human being who raises the seventh serpent converts oneself into a Maha-chohan.[38]

32. The spinal medulla penetrates the fourth ventricle of the brain, and after having passed through the third and fifth ventricle, reaches the chakra Sahasrara, which is situated in the superior part of the crown of the head.

33. The vertebral column has 33 vertebrae.

34. The cervical region is formed by seven vertebrae, the dorsal by twelve, the lumbar by five, the sacrum by five, and the coccygeal by four vertebrae.

35. These vertebrae are connected among themselves by fibro-cartilaginous cushions.

36. These vertebrae are septuple in their constitution, because they are in each one of the seven bodies of the human being.

37. Each one of these vertebrae corresponds, in the internal worlds, to a holy chamber.

___

37 See glossary.
38 Sanskrit for "Chief Lord." A title or rank.

Spinal Column

38. As the human being causes the Kundalini to rise throughout the spinal medulla, one is penetrating into each of the holy chambers of the temple.

39. Each of these 33 chambers is septuple in its internal constitution.

40. The seven aspects of each of these 33 holy chambers exactly correspond to the seven degrees of power of the fire.

41. With the first degree of power of the fire, we are penetrating within the first aspect of each one of these 33 holy chambers.

42. With the second degree of power of the fire, we penetrate within the second aspect of each one of these 33 holy chambers, which belong to the ethereal body.

43. With the third degree of power of the fire, we penetrate within the 33 holy chambers of the astral body.

44. We penetrate within the 33 holy chambers of the mental body with the fourth degree of power of the fire, and likewise successively.

45. We christify our seven bodies with the seven degrees of power of the fire.

46. With the seven degrees of power of the fire, we know the mysteries of the seven great Initiations of Major Mysteries.

47. Our entire personality must be absorbed within the Purusha.

48. Our entire personality must be absorbed within the Innermost.

49. The three Thrones must be awakened to liberty and life.

50. This is how we prepare ourselves to receive our resplendent Dragon of Wisdom, our Cosmic Chrestos, that incessant breath from the Absolute who lives within the depth of our Being.

51. The human being is converted into a Cosmic Chrestos when one receives one's resplendent Dragon of Wisdom.

52. Jesus of Nazareth converted himself into a Cosmic Chrestos when he received his resplendent Dragon of Wisdom in the Jordan.

53. John the Baptist was an initiate of the Cosmic Chrestos.

54. An eternal breath is within the heart of every life.

55. All of the breaths of life are the Great Breath emanated from the Absolute at the dawn of the mahamanvantara.

56. All the breaths are resplendent Dragons of Wisdom.

57. The Great Breath is the Cosmic Christ, the Army of the Voice,[39] Kwan-Yin,[40] the Melodious Voice,[41] Avalokiteshvara,[42] Vishnu,[43] Osiris,[44] the Central Sun.

58. After having raised the seven serpents upon the staff, the human being then, after some time of work, prepares to receive one's resplendent Dragon of Wisdom.

59. That is the "descent of Christ into the human being."

60. I, Aun Weor,[45] received my resplendent Dragon of Wisdom, named Samael, Logos of the planet Mars.

---

39 Elohim Sabbaoth (Hebrew), the army or host of gods and goddesses. "...the Dhyan Chohans, called Devas (gods) in India, or the conscious intelligent powers in Nature..." —HP Blavatsky, *The Secret Doctrine.* "Christ is not an individual but an army, the Army of the Voice, the Word." — Samael Aun Weor

40 Chinese 观音 "goddess of mercy," one of the many forms of Christ.

41 "The word of the gods."

42 Sanskrit अवलोकितेश्वर, deity who symbolizes the very embodiment of compassion.

43 Sanskrit वषिणु, the part of the Hindu trinity that sends his avatars into the world to help those who are suffering.

44 Egyptian god who gives all life.

45 It is necessary to understand the relationship between God, spirit, soul, and body. Samael Aun Weor is the bodhisattva (awakened human soul) of the Logos Samael, who is the Innermost Being. One thing is the human part, and another is the divine part. Samael Aun Weor is the name of the human soul (Tiphereth; Psykhe, Manas, the bodhisattva), who is not the same entity as the Innermost (Chesed, the Inner Buddha, Pneuma, Atman, Abraham), or what is commonly called "God," our "Father who is in secret" (Kether, the Logos, Brahma, Dharmakaya). Samael Aun Weor repeated many times that he, the terrestrial person, was no one important, but his inner Being is the archangel known by many names, such as Samael, Ares, Mars, etc., the Logos of the strength of Mars, that aspect of divinity that wages war against impurity and injustice.

61. "I am"[46] the Kalkian avatar of the new Aquarian era.

62. "I am" the Cosmic Christ of Aquarius.

63. "I am" the initiator of the new era.

64. "I am" Samael, the planetary genie of Mars.

---

46 Sanskrit सो ऽहम् Soham, "I am." Greek Ἐγώ εἰμι "I am" from εἶμαι. "I am" or
    "to be." A very common phrase in the Tantras, Upanishads, etc. making it
    a foundational expression of Vedic philosophy, and often used by Jesus.
    "Ἐγώ εἰμι [I AM] the way, the truth, and the life." —John 14:6. The "I am"
    indicates the profound nature of divinity as Being, which is far beyond
    "I," and is hidden in the symbolism of the swan found in Hindu and
    Greek myths. "... the Kalahansa, the Kala-ham-sa," and even the "Kali
    Hamsa," (Black swan)... Hamsa is equal to a-ham-sa, three words meaning
    "I am he" (in English), while divided in still another way it will read "So-
    ham," "he (is) I" — Soham being equal to Sah, "he," and aham, "I," or "I
    am he." —HP Blavatsky, *The Secret Doctrine*. "The Spirit of God floats upon
    the face of the waters." —Genesis 1:2. "Some people say, "I believe in the 'I
    want,' in the 'I can,' as well as in the 'I do.'" This is what they consider to
    be positive. But, in reality, these people fortify Satan with these affirma-
    tions. The Lamb [Christ] is not the "I." The Lamb is neither a superior
    "I," nor by a long shot an inferior "I." **When the Lamb says, "I AM,"
    we must interpret this as, "HE IS,"** because the Lamb is the one who is
    uttering it, and not the human being. [...] Some philosophers affirm that
    Christ brought the doctrine of the "I," because he said: "I AM the way, the
    truth, and the life." [John 14:6] Certainly, the Lamb said, "I AM," and only
    the Lamb can say "I AM." This phrase was spoken by the Lamb, but this
    phrase cannot be uttered by us (poor sinning shadows) because we are not
    the Lamb. Really, the exact and axiomatic translation of "I AM," which
    was uttered by the Lamb, must be as follows: "**HE IS** the way, the truth,
    and the life." "HE IS" because HE was the one who uttered it. We did not
    utter it; the one who uttered it was HIM, HIM, HIM. HE lives within the
    unknown profundities of our Being. "HE IS" the way, the truth, and the
    life. He transcends any concept of "I," any individuality, and any vestige of
    personality." —Samael Aun Weor, *The Aquarian Message*

Chapter 3

The Two Witnesses

1. *"And the angel that talked with me came again, and waked me, as a man that is wakened out of his sleep.*

2. *"And said unto me, What seest thou? And I said, I have looked, and behold a candlestick all of gold, with a bowl upon the top of it, and his seven lamps thereon, and seven pipes to the seven lamps, which are upon the top thereof:*

3. *"And two olive trees by it, one upon the right side of the bowl, and the other upon the left side thereof."* —Zechariah 4:1-3

4. *"Then answered I, and said unto him, What are these two olive trees upon the right side of the candlestick and upon the left side thereof?*

5. *"And I answered again, and said unto him, What be these two olive branches which through the two golden pipes empty the golden oil out of themselves?*

6. *"And he answered me and said, Knowest thou not what these be? And I said, No, my lord.*

7. *"Then said he, These are the two anointed ones, that stand by the Lord of the whole earth."* —Zechariah 4:11-14

8. The two olive branches that through the two golden pipes empty the golden oil out of themselves are the two nadis Ida and Pingala.

9. In the male, Ida rises from the right testicle and Pingala from the left testicle.

10. In the female, Ida rises from the left ovary and Pingala from the right ovary.[47]

---

47 "... everything in nature is based on the law of polarities. The right testicle finds its exact antipode in the left nasal cavity, as has already been demonstrated. The left testicle finds its perfect antipode in the right nasal cavity and obviously this is the way it must be. Esoteric physiology teaches us that in the feminine sex the two witnesses emerge from the ovaries. It is unquestionable that within women the order of these two olive trees of the temple is harmoniously reversed." —Samael Aun Weor, The Three Mountains

Ida and Pingala

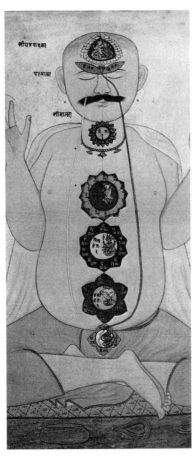

The two cords connecting the root of the nose with the Muladhara chakra. This is not literal anatomy, but a symbolic depiction of Ida and Pingala from Hindu Tantra.

In western alchemy, the two witnesses are represented by Adam and Eve, the two serpents on the caduceus of Mercury. They are rooted in the grail (the sexual organs). Atop the spinal column is Venus, the virgin Divine Mother, the Kundalini.

11. These (Ida and Pingala) are the two olive trees (of the temple), the two candlesticks standing before the God of the earth. These are the two witnesses, *"and if any man will hurt them, fire proceedeth out of their mouth and devoureth their enemies."* —Revelation 11:4, 5

12. The solar and lunar atoms of our seminal energy rise through these two ganglionic cords named Ida and Pingala.

13. In men, the right nasal cavity is related with Pingala. The left nasal cavity is related with Ida.

14. It is stated that in men the solar atoms enter through the right nasal cavity and that the lunar atoms enter through the left nasal cavity. In women, it is the opposite.

15. The yogis and yoginis who have not been initiated in the school of internal mysteries practice pranayama with the intention of attracting into the magnetic field of their nose millions of solar and lunar atoms from the exterior world.

16. However, the initiated yogi/yogini-esotericist does not search outside in the world of Maya.[48] The initiated yogi/ yogini-esotericist searches within the Self.

17. When an initiated yogi/yogini-esotericist practices pranayama, they only want to make their sexual energy rise from their testicles/ovaries to the sacred chalice of their brain.

18. Pranayama is an esoteric system in order to transmute the semen into Christic energy.

19. Pranayama is a system of transmutation for the sexual energy.

20. When the initiated yogi/yogini-esotericist inhales the Prana or Vital Christ through the right nasal cavity and exhales the Prana through the left nasal cavity, and vice versa, when one inhales through the left nasal cavity and exhales through the right nasal cavity, what one wants is not to attract external atoms as the profane believe,

---

48 Sanskrit माया Here used as "illusion, deception, appearance."

Pranayama

but rather, to raise the solar and lunar atoms from the testicles or ovaries to the magnetic field at the root of the nose.

21. The clairvoyant who observes the ganglionic cords Ida and Pingala of a yogi/yogini in the moments of practicing pranayama will see the pure waters of Amrita, the primordial waters of Genesis, ascending through these two nadis.

22. Swara[49] is the breathing science. Swara is the sacred science of respiration.

23. *"Ton-Sah-Ham are the mantras of inspiration. Ton Rah-Ham those of expiration whose ends [in the testes and ovaries] correspond to the rhythmic contraction and expansion of matter (undifferentiated cosmic, Prakriti, Mula-Prakriti)."*

24. *"After the mantra Swa-Ra is formed the sublime Swara, of which it is said in verse 15 of the Zhivagama: In the Swara are the Vedas and the Zastras (sacred books of the Hindus) —In the Swara is the highest Gandharva (celestial musician). In the Swara are the three worlds. The swara is the reflection of Parabrahman (the only absolute whole). That is why some authors exclaim: Swara is life and add: Swara is music...*

25. *"Swara later forms the basis of the Tattvas,[50] since these are the five modifications of the Great Breath."* —Huiracocha, Biorhythm

26. Now and then, the Great Breath is the Cosmic Christ, Avalokiteshvara, Kwan-Yin, the Melodious Voice, the Army of the Voice, whose head is a paramarthasatya[51] known in this humanity with the name of Jesus Christ.

---

49 or svara, Sanskrit स्वर "breath, sound, note." In yoga, regulation of breath. Swara is also the basis of music, since it refers to the sounds and names of musical notes. Since there are seven notes, swara indicates the number seven.

50 (Sanskrit) "truth, fundamental principle." A reference to the essential nature of a given thing. The Tattvas are the origin of fire, air, water, and earth.

51 Sanskrit परमार्थसत्य "asbsolute truth" from para, "absolute, supreme," parama, "that which knows, or the consciousness," artha, "that which is known," satya, "existence, Truth." In synthesis, "The supreme knowledge of all that exists: TRUTH." A being of very high development; an inhabitant of the Absolute.

27. Jesus Christ is the greatest initiate who has come into the world.

28. The Army of the Voice is the "Merkabah."[52] The coachman of that chariot is Jesus Christ, the divine Rabbi of Galilee.

29. Jesus Christ is an inhabitant of the Absolute who renounced the happiness of SAT,[53] the Unmanifested, to come into the world with swara, the reflection of Parabrahman.

30. Therefore, pranayama is the Christic science of the Great Breath or Cosmic Chrestos.

31. That great universal Breath of Life, the Cosmic Christ, abides within our Christonic semen.

32. When they are practicing pranayama, the yogi/yogini works with the Great Breath or Cosmic Chrestos that is deposited within the Christonic semen.

33. *"Pranayama (the practice that consists of taking deep breaths, holding the inspired air for as long as possible and then exhaling it until the lungs are empty) also teaches two poles of energy, one masculine and the other feminine. The first locates it in the brain (cerebrospinal system) and the other in the heart (sympathetic system). But just as by forming two poles in space, making a magnet work, we undoubtedly create new energies*

---

52 (Hebrew מרכבה, מֶרְכַּב, or מֶרְכָּבֶת) Literally, "thing to ride in, cart," interpreted to mean "chariot." Refers to the superior bodies that the initiate must build to reach "heaven." In Western mysticism, the chariot is most known in relation with Ezekiel, but is also symbolic in relation with Krishna, Apollo, and others.

53 (Sanskrit सत्) Literally, "existence, reality, truth, that which is, being, essence, enduring." Usually translated as "absolute existence," indicating the primordial emptiness or potentiality from which everything emerges and returns. "Brahman is Sat, the Absolute, Reality. That which exists in the past, present and future; which has no beginning, middle and end; which is unchanging and not conditioned by time, space and causation; which exists during the waking, dream and deep sleep states; which is of the nature of one homogeneous essence, is Sat. This is found in Brahman, the Absolute. The scriptures emphatically declare: "Only Sat was prior to the evolution of this universe." —Swami Sivananda

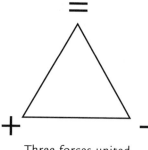

Three forces united

and the unconquered birth of a third pole is forced..." —Huiracocha, Biorhythm

We affirm that the third pole is Devi Kundalini, which, from the union of the solar and lunar atoms, is born within the Triveni,[54] situated in the coccyx.

34. These two polarities, masculine and feminine—from the Great Breath—prove the sexuality of Prana and Kundalini.

35. Kundalini is absolutely sexual.

36. People have the tendency of seeing sex as something filthy and horribly passionate. The yogi/yogini is ahead of Dsa, Ushti, Uste[55] (desire) and reverently prostrates before the Gnostic mysteries of sex, because they consider that sex is a sacred function of Devi Kundalini.

37. The yogi/yogini knows that the waters of Amrita (Christonic semen) are the habitat of fire.

38. The yogi/yogini knows that the entire force of the Solar Logos abides within the seed of any plant, animal and human.

39. The yogi/yogini knows that sex is a holy force and that it must not be corrupted with fornication.

40. The right nasal cavity in men is called Surya [sun] or Pingala. Respiration through this nostril causes the ascension of solar atoms from our seminal system.

---

54 Sanskrit त्रिवेणी "Triple-braided," the place where three holy rivers meet.

55 "Uste or Usta is the reason for desire as found in the Zend-Avesta."— Huiracocha, Biorhythm

41. The left nasal cavity is called Chandra [moon] or Ida. Respiration through this nostril causes the ascension of lunar atoms from our seminal system.

42. With exercises of pranayama, we reinforce the three breaths of pure akasha.[56] These three breaths are combined with the solar and lunar atoms of our seminal system to awaken Devi Kundalini.

43. Prana is the Vital Christ or Great Breath. That Vital Christ is modified into Akasha, within which is hidden the Son, the First Begotten, the Purusha of every human being.

44. Akasha is modified into ether, and the ether is transformed into tattvas. The tattvas are the origin of fire, air, water, and earth.

45. Therefore, everything that exists, everything that has been, and everything that shall be comes from the Great Breath, the Cosmic Christ, the Army of the Voice, whose supreme commander is Jesus Christ.

46. Paranishpanna (absolute happiness) without paramartha (awakened consciousness) is not happiness.

47. Jesus Christ attained paramartha and paranishpanna; nonetheless, he renounced the happiness of the Unmanifested Absolute to come and save human beings and gods.

---

56 Sanskrit आकाश "Space, sky, atmosphere, vacuity, ether, free or open space, subtle and ethereal fluid, heaven, god brahma." From akash, "to be visible, appear, shine, be brilliant." "According to the Hindu Philosophy the whole nature is composed of two principal substances. One of them is called the Akasa or ether and the other, Prana or energy. These two may be said to correspond to matter and force of the modern scientists. Everything in this universe that possesses form or that has material existence, is evolved out of this omnipresent and all-pervasive subtle substance 'Akasa'." —Swami Sivananda. The three breaths of pure Akasha descend through the Brahmanic cord into our body, where they manifest according to our sexual actions. Orgasm polarizes the forces to attract destructive elements. Chastity and transmutation polarize the forces to attract creative elements: ie. the awakening of Kundalini.

48. When the Elohim or glorious dhyanis[57] started to weave on the loom of God, they cried with pain when contemplating the twilight of the Uncreated Light that seemed to sink as a frightful setting sun.

49. Then Jesus Christ, the great paramarthasatya, passed through the dhyani-pasa[58] and came into the cosmic garden to save the gods, whose innumerable virginal sparks or jivas[59] are devolving and evolving during this mahakalpa.[60]

50. I, Samael Aun Weor, was a witness of all of these things. I saw when that great being entered the sanctuary and signed a pact of salvation for human beings and he crucified himself on his cross.

51. I witnessed the dawn of the mahamanvantara and give testimony of all of these things.

52. Later on, at the dawn of the fourth round, the master sent his buddha in order for him to prepare himself in this valley of tears. That buddha is his soul called Jesus.

53. And his Buddha lit his seven eternal lamps.

54. And his Buddha raised his seven serpents throughout the seven canals of the candlestick.

55. Thus, when his Buddha Jesus of Nazareth was prepared there in the Jordan, his resplendent Dragon of Wisdom entered within him in order to preach to human beings and gods.

56. The sacrifice already happened on that occasion. The commander of all Cosmic Christs, Jesus of Nazareth, already washed with his blood all the sins of the sanctuary and signed the pact between human beings

---

57 Literally "meditators," to mean awakened masters in the internal worlds.

58 "The rope of the Dhyanis or Spirits; the Pass-Not-Ring; the circle below which are all those who still labour under the delusion of seperateness." —Theosophical Glossary

59 Sanskrit जीव, literally "life, living being, the principle of life, vital breath, soul, existing, existence." A reference to the individual, embodied soul.

60 "Great expanse of time"

and Kwan-Yin, the Army of the Voice, Vishnu, Osiris, the Great Breath.

57. Jesus is the supreme conciliator between the human being and divinity.

58. The nadis Ida and Pingala are the subtle conductors of sukshma-prana,[61] the Christic sexual energy.

59. *"Ida and Pingala... meet with Sushumna Nadi at the chakra Muladhara...*

60. *"The junction of these three nadis at the Muladhara chakra is known as Mukta Triveni.. Again these three meet at the Anahata and Ajna chakras...*

61. *"Ida is cooling and Pingala is heating."*

62. *"Pingala digests the food.*

63. *"Ida is of pale, Sakti Rupa. It is the great nourisher of the world. Pingala is of fiery red, Rudra Rupa."* —Swami Sivananda, Kundalini Yoga

64. The yogi/yogini can retain the Prana that circulates through the nadi Sushumna at the point called Brahmarandhra, located in the frontal fontanel of newborn babies.

65. Thus, this is how the yogi/yogini can defy death and live entire ages.

66. However, this is only possible for the yogi/yogini that has received the Elixir of Long Life.

67. That elixir is a gas and a liquid.

68. That white-colored gas is electropositive and electronegative.

69. That gas remains deposited in the vital depth; thus the initiates can keep their physical bodies alive for millions of years.

70. This liquid makes the physical body subtle.

71. Thus, the physical body is absorbed within the ethereal body and becomes indestructible.

---

61 Astral prana.

72. The nadis Ida and Pingala are found side to side of the spinal medulla.

73. These nadis entwine around the spinal medulla in similar shape to the number eight.

74. The heavenly path is inside the nadi Sushumna.

75. The Kundalini ascends through Brahmanadi.

76. The Brahmanadi is found situated inside another very subtle canal that runs throughout the length of the spinal medulla and is known by the name Chitra.

77. The seven chakras known by the names Muladhara, Svadhisthana, Manipura, Anahata, Vishuddha, Ajna, and Sahasrara are over this nadi Chitra.

78. Buddhi (the Divine Soul) becomes united with Shiva (the Innermost) when the Kundalini reaches the chakra Sahasrara. This is the First Initiation of Major Mysteries.

The Spinal Cord and its Nadis

The physical spinal column has a hollow center that the spinal cord runs through. Within the spinal cord, there is a subtle energetic nadi called Sushumna. Within that, there is another called Vajra Nadi, which has solar, rajasic qualities. Within that, there is another called Chitra, which is sattvic and pale. Within that, there is another, very fine, called canalis centralis and Brahmanadi, through which the Kundalini rises.

Pranayama Exercise

79. Let the disciple sit on the ground, crossing one's legs in the oriental style. This position is called padmasana[62] in India.

80. Shut the left nasal cavity with the index finger and inhale the prana through the right nasal cavity.

81. Now, retain the air while shutting both nasal cavities with the index finger and the thumb.

82. Exhale the air through the left nasal cavity while shutting the right nasal cavity; inhale now through the left nasal cavity. Retain the air again and exhale through the right nasal cavity.

83. When you are inhaling the air, imagine the sexual energy ascending through the nadi related with the nasal cavity through which you are inhaling the prana.

84. When you are sending the inhaled prana downwards, think of the Three Breaths of pure Akash descending through the nadis Sushumna, Ida, and Pingala, to awake the chakra Muladhara where the Kundalini abides.

85. Prana is the purifying fire that cleans the scoria that plugs the nadis.

86. With the sexual transmutation of pranayama, the veils of rajas[63] and tamas[64] are dissipated.

87. With the practice of pranayama, the mind of the student is prepared for dharana, dhyana, and samadhi.

88. The disciple should practice pranayama ten minutes daily.

---

62 Sanskrit, "lotus posture." Most westerners cannot comfortably sit in full padmasana with the legs crossed and feet resting on the thighs. Easier variations rest one ankle on the floor, with the other leg on top of it. To ensure a straight back, most people need a cushion or bench to raise the hips higher than the knees. The most important aspects are to have a straight back and be perfectly relaxed.

63 Sanskrit रजस्, the guna related to passion, emotion, impurity.

64 Sanskrit तमस्, the guna related to ignorance, obscurity, heaviness, inertia

89. After finishing the practice, the disciple should drink a glass of milk or eat any light food.

90. Disciples can also practice while standing firmly on their feet.

91. The disciple should slowly inhale and exhale with one's mind very well concentrated in the practice of pranayama.

92. There are many asanas[65] and exercises of pranayama, but the former exercise of pranayama is enough for the transmutation of the student's sexual energies.

93. The disciples can also sit on a comfortable sofa to perform their practices.

94. Before starting one's practices, the disciple must pray to one's Innermost by meditating profoundly on Him.

95. The disciple must be profoundly concentrated on one's chakra Muladhara and begging to one's Purusha (the Innermost) for the awakening of the Kundalini.

96. Oriental Yoga gives a great variety of exercises for pranayama.

97. Let us see:

"...deep breathing exercise, Sukha Purvaka (easy comfortable) Pranayama during walking, Pranayama during meditation, Rhythmical breathing, Suryabheda, Ujjayi, Sitkari, Sitali, Bhastrika, Bhramari, Murchha, Plavini, Kevala Kumbhaka, etc." —Swami Sivananda, Kundalini Yoga

98. All of these innumerable varieties of practices and Asanas (postures) served for the descending arch of the evolving life; yet, now we are starting an ascending arch of evolution, and therefore, that enormous quantity of postures and exercises are antiquated for the new Aquarian era.

99. Now the yogis/yoginis of the new Aquarian era live a life of intense activity within the cities, and they do not need to withdraw into the solitary forests, because we are initiating the new Aquarian era. This era is of sociability, cooperation, and confraternity amongst all human beings

---

65 Sanskrit, postures.

without distinction of schools, races, sexes, castes, or religions.

100. All the exercises of pranayama can be executed in our home without too many complications, and without abandoning the execution of all the responsibilities with our family, society, and humanity.

101. The yogis/yoginis must be absolutely chaste, otherwise they will fail totally.

Chapter 4

The Yogic Matrimony

1. In our former chapter we studied the esotericism of pranayama and we realized that it is a scientific system of transmutation for celibate people (singles).

2. The swara (breathing science) is totally sexual.

3. The breathing science is reinforced by the sexual union of the spouses.

4. There is an act of Sexual Magic by means of which we can totally awaken and develop Devi Kundalini.

5. The formula is the following: introduce the virile member into the feminine vagina and withdraw from the sexual act without spilling the semen (without reaching the orgasm).

6. The refrained desire will transform the semen into light and fire.

7. The seminal vapors open the inferior orifice of the spinal medulla which in common and ordinary people is found completely closed.

8. This labor is developed under the direction of certain Devas[66] who govern the elemental department of the cedars[67] of the forest.

9. Devi Kundalini enters through the orifice of the nadi Sushumna.

10. Pranayama is totally reinforced with the practices of Sexual Magic.

11. The Great Breath is totally sexual.

12. Sexual Magic reinforces the Great Breath within us.

13. This is how Devi Kundalini evolves, develops, and progresses until attaining the union with the Lord Shiva.

---

66 Sanskrit "shining ones" gods, angels, etc.
67 Read *Igneous Rose* by Samael Aun Weor.

14. Gautama Buddha practiced his cult of Sexual Magic with his beautiful spouse Yasodhara.

15. Only the one who has drunk the juice of the plant of the moon (soma)[68] can be a Brahmin.

16. This plant of the moon is sex, whose juice (soma) awakens the Kundalini in us.

17. This is the secret of the Vedas.

18. The Master Helena Petrovna Blavatsky was a great yogini.

19. This great master, after having widowed, had to get married again in the last years of her life in order to attain her total realization and the development of all of her powers.

20. A certain disciple once asked the Master Morya, "Master, you already raised the seven serpents upon the staff; then why do you have a spouse?

    The master answered, "Because I got her before awakening my fires, and I need her to enliven my fires."

21. The refrained desire makes our sexual energies rise through Ida and Pingala; thus, finally, the lunar and solar atoms from Ida and Pingala join in the triveni to awaken Devi Kundalini.

22. During amorous caresses, the electricity and universal fire of life are accumulated in our atmosphere.

23. If human beings ejaculate their semen, then, like electric batteries, they discharge themselves and totally fail in the Great Work of the Father.

24. The refrained desire causes the transmutation of the seminal liquor into Christic energy that rises through the nadis Ida and Pingala.

25. The yogi/yogini withdraws from their spouse before the spasm or orgasm to avoid the seminal ejaculation.

26. The seminal fire ascends through the nadi Sushumna throughout the length of the Brahmanadi.

---

68 Sanskrit सोम, the sacred drink of the gods (i.e. amrita, ambrosia).

27. This is how the esotericist-yogi/yogini realizes their Self totally, in depth, as masters of the cosmic day, as masters of the mahamanvantara.

28. The yogis/yoginis of the new Aquarian era realize their Self through the sexual act.

29. The times are gone in which yogis needed to withdraw into the jungle to practice their esoteric exercises.

30. Now yogis realize their Self though the sexual act.

31. The motto of the new Aquarian era is human cooperation.

32. Yogis must live within society, serving their brothers and sisters, and living with happiness and optimism.

33. The new Aquarian era does not admit hermit-yogis.

34. The Age of Maitreya[69] is the age of association and confraternity among all human beings.

35. Sex is terrifically divine, and therefore the yogi/yogini must clean their mind from all kind of desires and animal passions.

36. The person who looks at sex with repugnance defiles the terrific secret of the Vedas and the science of the Great Breath, contained in the Vedas and the Shastras.

37. The yogi/yogini who flees from the sacred mysteries of sex is still filled with desires and animal passions.

38. Angels see sex with the eyes of an angel; yet, demons see sex with the eyes of a demon, even when they dress themselves with the sheepskin and disguise themselves as saints.

39. The yogi/yogini forms their home without the necessity of violating the sixth commandment[70] of the law of God: "Thou shall not fornicate."

40. During the act of Sexual Magic a single sperm can escape. The [divine] lunar hierarchies[71] can select that sperm to

---

69 Another name for the new Aquarian era.

70 The order of commandments relates to the sephiroth of the Tree of Life.

71 The Moon is the first of the seven classical planets, and is responsible for beginnings, conception, birth, creation, new evolutions, etc.

fecundate the womb without the necessity of spilling the semen.

41. This is how the Lemurians engendered their children on the stony sacred patios of their temples.

42. The tenebrous ones from the [devolving] lunar path[72] were the ones who taught human beings how to ejaculate their seminal liquor. This is how human beings sank into the darkness.

43. Now, we have to return into the sacred conception of the Holy Spirit.

44. The children of the yogi and yogini are fragments of victory, children of chastity, children engendered by Kriya-shakti.[73]

45. All yogis and yoginis must love their spouse and their children, and live amidst harmony, music, love, and beauty.

46. Love dignifies; love exalts the soul.

47. God shines upon the perfect couple.

48. There is nothing greater than love. Man and woman were born to love each other.

49. The true yogi and yogini convert their home into an Eden[74] of ineffable joys.

50. The divine priestess is the woman of the yogi, and vice versa.

51. By means of the very sweet enchantment of love, women convert men into ineffable gods, and vice versa.

52. Yogis and yoginis realize their Selves by means of love. This is better than carrying out the life of a hermit.

---

72 Here, lunar refers to the left-hand path, the path of black magic, and an event that occurred in the Lemurian era, symbolized by the story of Adam and Eve in the Judeo-Christian scriptures. Read *The Elimination of Satan's Tail* by Samael Aun Weor.

73 (Sanskrit) "Creation by will." Comprised of kriya, "activity," and shakti, "intelligent energy," specifically related to the Divine Mother (Binah: intelligence). The resulting term Kriyashakti implies how will / consciousness creates by directing energy.

74 Hebrew , "bliss, happiness."

Chapter 5
The Chakra Muladhara

1. As the Kundalini ascends within the Nadi Chitra, each of the chakras located along the spinal medulla awakens.
2. These seven chakras are located along the spinal medulla.
3. When the Kundalini is still enclosed within the Muladhara chakra, the seven chakras hang downwards.
4. However, when Devi Kundalini ascends through Brahmanadi, then the marvelous petals of these chakras turn upward towards Brahmarandhra, marvelously gleaming with the incomparable sexual fire of Kundalini.
5. Today, in this lesson, we are going to study the Muladhara chakra.
6. This chakra resides at the very base of the spinal column, and is located between the sexual organs and the anus.
7. So this chakra is located at the very root of our genital organs. It awakens in the man and in the woman when they unite their enchantment in Sexual Magic.
8. The yogi/yogini who does not have a spouse can activate the flames of Kundalini with pranayama and meditation. However, the complete, total, and absolute development of the seven degrees of power of the fire is only possible when practicing Sexual Magic with our priest/priestess-spouse.
9. This is why the yogini Helena Petrovna Blavatsky had to marry again in the last years of her life, long after her first husband Count Blavatsky died.
10. The seven chakras are the seven churches mentioned in the book Revelation of Saint John.
11. Now, we are studying the Muladhara chakra; this is the church of Ephesus.
12. *"Unto the angel of the church of Ephesus write: These things saith he that holdeth the seven stars in his right hand, who walketh in the midst of the seven golden candlesticks."* —Revelation 2:1

Muladhara Chakra

ROOT

SANSKRIT NAME: MULADHARA
GREEK NAME: EPHESUS
TIBETAN NAME: BLISS

DEVA / DEVATA: Dakini (Shakti)
POWERS: Awakening of Kundalini
REGION: Coccyx / sexual organs
SEED MANTRA: ल (lam)
TATTVA: Prithvi / Earth
VIRTUES REQUIRED: Patience
VOWEL: S, pronounced "ss"

13. The one who walks in the midst of the seven golden candlesticks is our inner Christ, our inner angel.

14. The seven golden candlesticks are the seven spinal medullas, which are interrelated with our seven bodies.

15. The sacred fire ascends throughout these seven spinal medullas.

16. So, each one of our seven bodies has its own golden candlestick; that is to say, each one has its spinal medulla and its sacred fire.

17. We have seven serpents: two groups of three, with the sublime coronation of the seventh tongue of fire that unite us with the One, with the Law, with the Father.

18. The seven stars that our inner Christ has in his right hand are the seven chakras of our spinal medulla.

19. *"The Muladhara chakra is located... just below the Kanda and the junction where Ida, Pingala and Sushumna Nadis meet."*
    —Swami Sivananda, Kundalini Yoga

20. This is the fundamental or coccygeal chakra. This chakra nourishes all the other chakras with its sexual energy.[75]

21. The Kundalini is enclosed within the Muladhara chakra.
    "From this Chakra four important Nadis emanate which appear as petals of a lotus." —Swami Sivananda, Kundalini Yoga

22. The seven levels of cosmic consciousness are situated underneath the church of Ephesus.[76]

23. The mantra of this chakra is **Bhur**.[77]

24. The mantras **Dis**, **Das**, **Dos** must be vocalized by prolonging the sound of the vowels and letter **S**.

---

75 "This is the Adhara Chakra (support) as the other Chakras are above this. Kundalini, which gives power and energy to all the Chakras, lies at this Chakra. Hence this, which is the support of all is called Muladhara or Adhara Chakra." —Swami Sivananda, Kundalini Yoga

76 "The seven Underworlds: Atala, Vitala, Sutala, Talatala, Rasatala, Mahatala and Patala Lokas are below this Chakra." —Swami Sivananda, Kundalini Yoga

77 Sanskrit भूर "earth."

25. When vocalized in Sexual Magic, the mantras **Dis**, **Das**, **Dos** awaken the Kundalini.

26. *"I know thy works, and thy labor, and thy patience, and how thou canst not bear them which are evil; and thou hast tried them which say they are Apostles, and are not, and hast found them liars."* —Revelation 2:2

27. The root of good and evil is found in the church of Ephesus.

28. There are many who say they are apostles but are not, because they are fornicators.

29. *"Remember, therefore, from whence thou art fallen, and repent, and do the first works; or else I will come unto thee quickly and will remove thy candlestick out of it's place, except thou repent and sadness will afflict thy heart."* —Revelation 2:5

30. When the human being ejaculates the semen (reaches the orgasm), the Kundalini descends one or more vertebrae in accordance with the magnitude of the fault.

31. Thus, *"I will remove thy candlestick out of his place, except thou repent."*

32. To re-conquer the power of the vertebrae lost in one ejaculation is very hard and difficult.

33. This is why our Lord the Christ told me, "The disciple must not let oneself fall, because the disciple who lets oneself fall has to struggle very hard to recover what one has lost."

34. *"He that hath an ear, let him hear what the Spirit saith unto the churches: To him that overcometh will I give to eat of the Tree of Life which is in the midst of the Paradise of God."* — Revelation 2:7

35. There are two trees:[78] the Tree of the Science of Good and Evil,[79] and the Tree of Life.[80]

36. The Tree of the Science of Good and Evil is the sexual force.

37. The Tree of Life is the inner Christ of each human being.

38. The Tree of the Science of Good and Evil must be transformed into the Immolated Lamb of the Heavenly Jerusalem.

39. This is only possible when we inebriate ourselves with the aroma of that forbidden fruit that is pleasant to the sight and of a delectable aspect, of which God said, *"Thou shalt not eat of it: for in the day that thou eatest thereof thou shalt surely die."*

40. We must always withdraw from our spouse before the orgasm; thus, we avoid the seminal ejaculation. This is how the chakra Muladhara awakens. This is how Devi Kundalini awakens.

41. This is how we transform the Tree of Science of Good and Evil into the Immolated Lamb.

42. This is how we transform into living Christs, and we eat of the Tree of Life that is in the midst of the paradise of our God.

43. The Muladhara chakra is related with the Tattva Prithvi. Whosoever totally awakens this chakra and attains in-depth realization can receive the Elixir of Long Life and preserve the physical body for millions of years.

44. The Kundalini grants us knowledge of the past, present, and future.

---

78 "And out of the ground made the LORD God to grow every tree that is pleasant to the sight, and good for food; the **tree of life** also in the midst of the garden, and the **tree of knowledge** of good and evil." — Genesis 2:9

79 Hebrew, עץ "tree," דעת Daath "knowledge," טוב "goodness," רע "pollution, impurity." Daath is related to sexuality, known also as Alchemy and Tantra. The full name indicates that sexual "knowledge," leads to either "goodness" or "impurity."

80 Hebrew עץ החיים "tree of lives," related to the laws and structures of existence; also called Kabbalah, metaphysics, numerology, mathematics, etc.

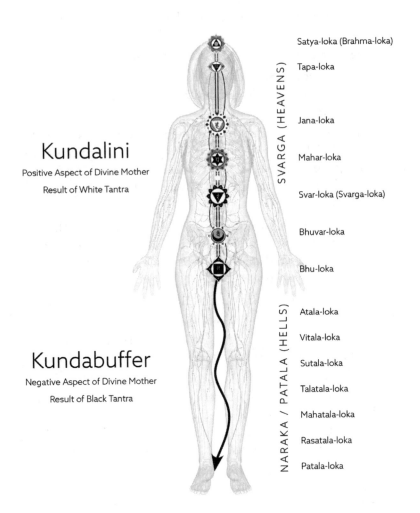

Kundalini

Positive Aspect of Divine Mother

Result of White Tantra

Kundabuffer

Negative Aspect of Divine Mother

Result of Black Tantra

Satya-loka (Brahma-loka)

Tapa-loka

Jana-loka

Mahar-loka

Svar-loka (Svarga-loka)

Bhuvar-loka

Bhu-loka

SVARGA (HEAVENS)

Atala-loka

Vitala-loka

Sutala-loka

Talatala-loka

Mahatala-loka

Rasatala-loka

Patala-loka

NARAKA / PATALA (HELLS)

Kundalini and Kundabuffer

45. In India, there is an evil order called Kula, of the tenebrous goddess Kali.[81] This is an order of black magic.

46. These dismal yogis/yoginis fornicate; they ejaculate their semen; they violate the sixth commandment of the law of God. This is how they negatively awaken their Kundalini.

47. When the yogi/yogini ejaculates their semen, then the Kundalini descends one or more vertebrae in accordance with the magnitude of their fault.

48. During their practices of negative Sexual Magic, the black magicians ejaculate their semen.

49. Millions of solar atoms are lost in the ejaculation of the seminal fluid. These solar atoms are replaced by billions of satanic atoms collected from the inner atomic infernos of the human being. These satanic atoms are collected by means of the peristaltic spasmic movements of the sexual organs after fornication (after the orgasm).

50. The satanic atoms intend to ascend through the Brahmanic cord; however, the three Akashic breaths precipitate them downward to the coccyx towards the Muladhara chakra.

51. Then a certain atom in the Muladhara chakra enters into activity. Thus the Kundalini, instead of going upward throughout the Brahmanadi, goes downward to the atomic infernos of the human being and forms in the astral body the tail (the Kundabuffer organ) with which Satan is represented.

52. During the act of Sexual Magic, the three pure Akashic breaths are reinforced by human will; thus, for us they can be a blessing or a curse.

53. If the yogi/yogini ejaculates their semen, then they will convert themselves into tenebrous tantric personalities of the lunar path.

---

81 Kali, symbolic spouse of Shiva, has positive and negative aspects, and is therefore utilized by both white and black magic.

54. Those tantric personalities are totally separated from their Purusha; that is to say, they are totally separated from their Innermost or Jivatma.

55. Every personality who is separated from their Innermost sinks themselves into the lunar abysses, and little by little they disintegrate within the most terrible desperation. This is the Second Death cited in the book Revelation of Saint John.

56. But when the yogi/yogini withdraws from their spouse before the spasm, then the solar and lunar atoms multiply themselves and ascend through the nadis Ida and Pingala upward to the chalice (the encephalon).

57. Finally, the solar and lunar atoms meet in the coccyx; then the three pure Akashic breaths that descend throughout the sacred rod (spine) of the yogi/yogini awaken Devi Kundalini, so that they may raise her throughout the Brahmanadi.

58. The bamboo reed symbolizes our spinal column.

59. Thus this is how the moment arrives in which Devi Kundalini and the Lord Shiva become united in order to transform us into masters of high mysteries of the great white universal brotherhood.[82]

60. Thus the woman (Maya-Shakti) is the door into Eden; let us love her! Blessed be the woman (Maya-Shakti)![83]

---

82 The ancient collection of pure human beings who uphold and propagate the highest and most sacred of sciences. It is called "white" due to its purity and cleanliness (ie. the absence of pride, lust, anger, etc.). This "brotherhood" or "lodge" includes men and women of the highest order from every race, culture, creed and religion. "There are masters from all races in our venerable White Lodge... God has no preference for anyone. All human beings without distinction of sex, race, creed, or color are beloved children of the Father. They have the same rights." —Samael Aun Weor, *Igneous Rose*

83 Maya-shakti is an epithet of the Divine Mother, the power of divinity within us that awaits its activation.

Chapter 6
The Chakra Svadhishthana

1. The Kundalini passes through chakra after chakra.

2. This is how the different states of consciousness are opened. This is how the sadhaka[84] penetrates all the states of cosmic consciousness until finally acquiring the awakening of Absolute Consciousness.

3. The yogi/yogini acquires multiple siddhis (powers) in accordance with the awakening of one's superlative consciousness.

4. In the internal worlds the word *time* is a synonym of esoteric degrees of consciousness.

5. There are eighteen initiations: nine Initiations of Minor Mysteries and nine Initiations of Major Mysteries.

6. When in the internal worlds we state that a brother is ten years old, we are simply affirming that he is an initiate of the first Minor Mystery.

7. When we affirm that a disciple is ninety years old, we are asseverating that he is an initiate of the ninth initiation of Minor Mysteries.

8. When we state that a brother is one hundred years old, we are affirming that he is in the first initiation of Major Mysteries.

9. The ages of more than nine hundred years are Logoic ages.

10. Experience has taught us that any master who has not yet reached the fundamental root of the hierarchy, that is to say, that has not yet reached the ninth initiation of Major Mysteries, is very weak. That master does not yet possess that strong and unbendable moral structure of those who already have reached Logoic ages.

---

84 Sanskrit साधक "worshiper, achiever, magician, adept, perfecting, proving"

11. In order to have the right to enter into the Absolute, it is necessary to possess the age of 300,000 divine years.

12. The last cape that a Logos wears is the Starry Mantle, with which he gains the right to enter into the Absolute.

13. Chronological time does not exist; what does exist is esoteric time, because life is an eternal instant.

14. All mudras and bandhas[85] are totally useless for the new Aquarian era.

15. What are the mudras useful for? It is important to transmute the sexual energies by means of love, poetry, music, and through unselfish service to this wretched suffering humanity.

16. Yet, to insert a silver tube with water into the urethra, as suggested in one of the mudras, only destroys the sexual organs, wherein is the key to redemption.

17. A yogi/yogini can live with their physical body for millions of years and move about within the pure Akasha without the necessity of cutting the inferior tendon of his tongue, as the Khechari mudra unfortunately teaches.

18. What is important is to attain the Elixir of Long Life and to become strong with the practice of internal meditation.

19. Gray hair and wrinkles disappear from the yogi/yogini without the necessity of performing difficult postures, such as standing on one's shoulders, raising the legs while holding the buttocks with the hands, as unfortunately is shown in the Sarvangasana mudra.

20. What is important is to be pure and chaste in order to vanquish old age and death.

21. Most of all, mudras are inadequate for the new Aquarian era. It is not necessary to suffocate the Kundalini by

---

85 Mudras and Bandhas are yogic postures. The most common are Mula Bandha, Jalandhara Bandha, Uddiyana Bandha, Maha Mudra, Maha Bandha, Maha Vedha, Yoga Mudra, Viparitakarani Mudra, Khechari Mudra, Vajroli Mudra, Shakti Chalana Mudra, Yoni Mudra

holding the breath too much in order to awaken it; a short breath during pranayama is enough.

22. The Kundalini awakens when we love our spouse and when following the path of the most absolute sanctity, when loving all living beings, and when we sacrifice ourselves in the Great Work of the Father.

23. What the human being needs is upright actions, upright thoughts, and upright feelings; conscientious action, conscientious word, and conscientious feeling.

24. What is important is to live life intensely in order to awaken the consciousness and to attain great realizations.

25. What is the use of standing on one's head as Urdhva-Padmasana[86] teaches?

26. What is best is to finish with our moral defects and to sacrifice ourselves for this humanity that suffers in this "valley of tears."

27. I, Samael Aun Weor, planetary Logos of Mars, say to my arhats: what is best is to love, because the force of love will take us to the ineffable joy of the Absolute, where life free in its movement palpitates.

28. The Svadhishthana chakra is the abode of the tattva Apas.

29. The elemental genie Varuna[87] is intimately related with this chakra.

30. The color of this chakra shines with the fire of Kundalini.

31. This chakra has six marvelous petals.

32. The mantra of this chakra is **Bhuvar**.

33. The yogi/yogini who meditates in this chakra never fears water; one learns to command the elemental creatures of the waters and conquers hidden powers.

34. With the awakening of this chakra the yogi/yogini learns to recognize the different kinds of astral entities.

---

86 A headstand with the legs folded in the lotus posture.
87 Sanskrit वरुण, Hindu deity of sky and water.

Svadhishthana Chakra

PROSTATE / UTERUS
SANSKRIT NAME: SVADHISHTHANA
GREEK NAME: SMYRNA
TIBETAN NAME: SECRET

DEVA / DEVATA: Brahma and Rakini

POWERS: Creation, sexual control, consciousness of internal worlds, power in practical magic

REGION: Prostate / uterus

SEED MANTRA: व (vam)

TATTVA: Apas / Water

VIRTUES REQUIRED: Chastity (Brahmacharya)

VOWEL: M, pronounced "mm"

35. With the awakening of this chakra the yogi/yogini conquers death.

36. This chakra awakens the prostatic plexus which is fundamental in the performance of practical magic.

37. An extraordinary, beautiful crescent moon is within this chakra.

38. This chakra controls the kidneys, the abdomen, and the principal organs of the lower part of the abdomen.

39. In the book Revelation of Saint John, this chakra is known as the church of Smyrna.

40. *"I know thy works and thy tribulations, and thy poverty, and I know the blasphemy of them which say they are Jews, and are not, but are the synagogue of Satan.*

41. *"Fear none of these things which thou shall suffer: behold, the devil shall cast some of you into prison, that ye may be tried; and ye shall have tribulation ten days; be thou faithful unto death and I will give thee a crown of life.*

42. *"He that hath an ear, let him hear what the Spirit saith unto the churches; he that overcometh shall not be hurt of the Second Death."* —Revelation 2:9-11

43. The Second Death is for fornicators. The Tantric personalities who follow the lunar path separate themselves from their Innermost, or Purusha, and sink themselves into the sublunar spheres where they disintegrate little by little.

44. The Kula order of the tenebrous goddess Kali came from Atlantis and passed into India. This is an order of black magic.

45. There are two types of magicians in that order: those who hate sex and those who do not, but during their negative Sexual Magic rites they practice "mystical" ejaculation. Some of their tenebrous partisans have made this negative tantra known in the western world.

46. Those who hate the sexual force hate the Great Breath because the Great Breath is the same sexual force. The Great Breath is the Christic sexual force and those who

hate this force hate the Christ. Therefore, they place themselves, in fact, on the path of black magic.

47. Our disciples are tempted and have to suffer "tribulation for ten days." One has to suffer to realize the ten sephiroth in oneself.

48. These are the ten sephiroth of Kabbalah. Whosoever wants to self-realize the ten sephiroth and convert their Self into a Christ has to be faithful unto death. Thus, "I will give thee a crown of life." The Inner Christ is the incessant Eternal Breath who dwells within us.

Chapter 7
The Chakra Manipura

1. Manipura is the third chakra of our spinal medulla.

2. This chakra of our spinal medulla resides in the Nabhi Sthana (the navel area).

3. The hepatic and splenic plexuses enter into activity when this chakra awakens.

4. Ten yoga nadis emanate from this chakra.

5. The color of this chakra is like a resplendent fire.

6. The tattva Tejas is intimately related with this marvelous chakra.

7. The deity that rules this chakra is Vishnu, and the goddess Lakshmi[88] is also intimately related with this marvelous lotus.

8. The mantra ₹ **Ram**[89] awakens this marvelous chakra. The sound of each letter must be prolonged as follows: *rrrrrrrrraaaaaaaaammmmmmmmm.*

9. Our disciples could invoke the god Agni[90] so that Agni can help them to awaken this marvelous chakra.

10. The god Agni has the appearance of a newborn baby, and when he presents himself dressed in formal attire, he wears a marvelous ornamented crystalline tunic.

11. Then we see the countenance of this portentous being as ineffable lightning.

12. The aura of Agni produces light and music.

13. Agni, the god of fire, restores the igneous powers in each of our seven bodies.

---

88 Sanskrit लक्ष्मी one of the three primary aspects of the Divine Mother. Lakshmi is the wife / feminine aspect — meaning the shakti, power — of Vishnu, the preserver or restorer, the Second Logos.

89 This is the bija (seed mantra) of Agni, fire.

90 Sanskrit अग्नि One of the most ancient symbols in the world, representing the source and power of the sun, lightning, and fire. The Rig Veda states that all the gods are centered in Agni (fire).

Manipura Chakra

SOLAR PLEXUS
SANSKRIT NAME: MANIPURA
GREEK NAME: PERGAMOS
TIBETAN NAME: CONJURATION

DEVA / DEVATA: Vishnu and Lakshmi

POWERS: Telepathy

REGION: Solar plexus

SEED MANTRA: र (ram)

TATTVA: Tejas / Fire

VIRTUES REQUIRED: Control of emotion, chastity, loyalty, faith, and obedience to the Father

VOWEL: U, pronounced "ew"

14. The mantra **Swa!** is pronounced as follows:
    Suuuuuuuuuaaaaaaaaaaaaaaa... sua!

15. The yogi/yogini who learns to meditate on this chakra
    attains Patala siddhi,[91] great occult powers, and is free
    from any type of sickness.

16. This chakra is the telepathic center or emotional brain.

17. The mental waves of people who think of us reach the
    solar plexus; thereafter those waves pass into our brain.

18. Therefore, the solar plexus is our receiving antenna.

19. Our pineal gland is our transmitting center.

20. This chakra collects the solar forces and nourishes all the
    other plexuses with them.

21. The yogi/yogini who awakens this chakra acquires the
    sense of telepathy.

22. The yogi/yogini who awakens this chakra will never fear
    fire and will be able to remain alive within the flames.

23. The constitution of our vertebral column is marvelous.

24. Indeed, the vertebrae are placed one above the other,
    forming a very beautiful pillar upon which not only our
    cranium is supported but our entire marvelous organism.

25. Our spinal column is a marvelous clavichord that we
    have to learn how to play in order to bring forth all the
    enchanted melodies of the zodiac.

26. There are marvelous gaps between each pair of vertebrae
    so that the spinal nerves can pass through them. These
    spinal nerves come from our spinal medulla to join each
    one of the prodigious chakras of the grand sympathetic
    nervous system.

27. The yogi/yogini must keep the elasticity of the spinal
    column.

---

91 "Yogi becomes Lord of desire, destroys sorrows and diseases." —Swami
Sivananda, *Kundalini Yoga*

Practice

28. Standing on our feet, vertical posture, with the hands placed on the waist, the yogi/yogini will turn the trunk from right to left at the waist, and thus will keep the elasticity of the spinal column.

29. The solar plexus is the seat of Satan[92] (inferior astral lunar body).

30. The Revelation of Saint John warns us as follows:

    "I know thy works and where thou dwellest, even where Satan's seat is: and thou holdest fast my name, and hast not denied my faith, even in those days wherein Antipas was my faithful martyr, who was slain among you, where Satan dwelleth.

    "But I have a few things against thee, because thou hast there them that hold the doctrine of Balaam, who taught Balac to cast a stumblingblock before the children of Israel, to eat things sacrificed unto idols, and to commit fornication.

    "So hast thou also them that hold the doctrine of the Nicolaitans, which thing I hate. Repent; or else I will come unto thee quickly, and will fight against them with the sword of my mouth.

    "He that hath an ear, let him hear what the Spirit saith unto the churches; To him that overcometh will I give to eat of the hidden manna, and will give him a white stone, and in the stone a new name written, which no man knoweth saving he that receiveth it." —Revelation 2:13 -17

31. The lunar body or inferior astral body—called Satan in esoteric Christian language—is connected to the solar plexus.

32. Now our disciples will comprehend from where the desires of overeating and drinking alcohol come.

33. Now our brothers and sisters will understand where the craving for fornication and gluttony is born.

34. The lunar body is a remnant from our animal past.

35. The ancestral inheritance from the animal kingdom is preserved as our lower passions within the lunar body.

---

92 Hebrew "adversary," our egos, defects, vices, etc.

36. When we were animal elementals, our astral lunar (protoplasmic) body was not yet divided.

37. Yet, when we entered the human kingdom for the first time, this astral lunar body was divided in two portions. The superior part was imbibed by the mind (inferior manas); during sleep, any yogi/yogini moves consciously [out of the physical body] with this part. The other, the inferior, is called Satan in the esoteric Christian language; this is the inferior lunar astral body (Kama-rupa).

38. In perverse personalities, this lunar body is gigantic and deformed.

39. Now our brothers and sisters will understand why our Lord the Christ said,

    "Except ye be converted, and become as little children, ye shall not enter into the kingdom of heaven." —Matthew 18:3

40. Satan is nourished with our appetites and passions. Yet, when we remove the sources of his nutrition, he becomes smaller and beautiful.

41. This is how, dear brothers and sisters, we eat of hidden manna,[93] the bread of wisdom.

42. This is how, beloved disciples, we receive the cornerstone[94] from the temple of the living God.

43. That cornerstone is our resplendent Dragon of Wisdom, our inner Christ; that is the Breath of the Central Sun within us.

44. This is the small white stone on which is written our holy name.

45. Repent, dear brothers and sisters, and finish with all your defects.

---

93 Hebrew מָן "sustenance from above," a holy form of "bread" given to the Israelites when they were in the desert.

94 "Therefore thus saith the Lord GOD, Behold, I lay in Zion for a foundation a stone, a tried stone, a precious corner stone, a sure foundation: he that believeth shall not make haste." —Bible, Isaiah 28:16

46. Sanctify yourselves, brothers and sisters of my soul, so that you will not fall into the lunar abysses (Avitchi).[95]

47. Perverse personalities are divorced from the Monad[96] and sink themselves into the lunar abysses of the eighth sphere.[97]

---

95 (Sanskrit and Pali, literally "without waves"; also transliterated Avichi, Avici) In Buddhism, the lowest level of the hell realms, inhabited by those who have committed one or more of the Five Grave Offenses:
   - Intentional murder of one's father (including our inner Father, who is "killed" when we fall from the path)
   - Intentional murder of one's mother (including our inner Mother, who is "killed" when we fall from the path)
   - Killing an arhat (enlightened being, including within us)
   - Harming a Buddha (including our inner Buddha)
   - Creating a division or split within the spiritual community (including within ourselves)

96 From Latin monas, "unity; a unit" and Greek monas "unit," from monos "alone." In general use, the Monad refers to the Being, the Innermost, our own inner Spirit. In Kabbalah, the Monad is represented by the sephiroth Chesed, Geburah, and Tiphereth. In Sanskrit, this corresponds to Atman-Buddhi-Manas.

97 In hell (Klipoth), the eighth infernal circle, the sphere of Uranus. "... within the eighth infernal circle unluckily dwell the false alchemists, the devotees of Black Tantra, the falsifiers of metal (Mercury, sexual power). They are those who crystallized negatively. To be more precise, they are those who, instead of crystallizing the Sexual Hydrogen Ti-12 in the superior existential bodies of the Being, made it crystallize negatively...."
—Samael Aun Weor, *Hell, the Devil, and Karma*

Chapter 8
The Chakra Anahata

1. This chakra has complete control over the heart plexus.
2. Its color is like living fire.
3. Indeed, there is a jet-black hexagonal space inside this marvelous chakra.
4. This chakra is intimately related with the Tattva Vayu.[98]
5. The deity that rules this chakra is Isha, who controls and rules this chakra along with the Devata Kakini.
6. The Bana Linga[99] is intimately related with the Anahata chakra.
7. The Svayambhu Linga is intimately related with the Muladhara chakra.
8. The Anahata sound, or the Shabda Brahman sound, resounds within this marvelous chakra of the Nadi Sushumna.
9. This marvelous sound is the sound of the Fohat.
10. The sound of the Fohat is the "S" which is vocalized as follows: Sssssssssss... as a sweet and affable whistle.
11. The yogi/yogini who learns how to meditate in this chakra will become an absolute master of the Tattva Vayu and will be able to dissolve hurricanes and command the winds at will.
12. Some yogis state that one can float in the air and penetrate into the body of another person just by meditating on this chakra.
13. Undoubtedly, to float in the air and to penetrate into the body of another person is very easy; it can be accomplished by anybody, even if one is a beginner in these studies.
14. To float in the air is as easy as drinking a cup of water.

---

98 The subtle source of air.
99 Sanskrit "mark, sign, symbol" representative of Shiva, the Third Logos.

Anahata Chakra

HEART
SANSKRIT NAME: ANAHATA
GREEK NAME: THYATIRA
TIBETAN NAME: DHARMA

DEVA / DEVATA: Isha (Rudra) and Kakini

POWERS: Inspiration, presentiment, intuition, astral travel, jinn travel

REGION: Heart

SEED MANTRA: य (yam)

TATTVA: Vayu / Air

VIRTUES REQUIRED: Conscious love, charity, service, faith, patience

VOWEL: O, pronounced "oh"

15. The secret is very simple; it is enough for the disciple to learn how to penetrate into the astral plane[100] with one's physical body.

Practice

16. Disciples must slumber lightly; then very softly they must get up from their bed as if they were somnambulists; that is to say, preserving the sleepy state as a very precious treasure.

17. Thus, in this way, the disciple walks like a somnambulist, and filled with faith, they will jump with the intention of floating in the surrounding environment.

18. If the disciple achieves floating in the air, it is because the physical body has penetrated the astral plane. Thus, the disciple can go through space and soar to any given place on Earth.

19. This is how we can fly with the physical body within the astral plane.

20. While the physical body is inside the astral plane it becomes submitted to the laws of the astral plane but without losing its physiological characteristics.

21. Therefore, to float in the air with the physical body can be done by anyone. What is important is to have faith, tenacity, and very much patience.

22. The fires of the heart control the spinal fires.

23. The fires of the heart control the ascent of the Kundalini.

24. The ascent of the Kundalini happens in accordance with the merits of our heart.

25. In order to get the benefit of only one vertebra in the spinal column, the yogi must submit to numerous trials and terrible purifications.

26. The progress, development, and evolution of the Kundalini is very slow and difficult.

---

100 The fifth dimension, the world of dreams. Sanskrit सूक्ष्म sukshma.

27. With only one seminal ejaculation [orgasm], the Kundalini descends one or more vertebrae in accordance with the magnitude of the fault.

28. To re-conquer the powers of those vertebrae is terribly difficult.

29. The serpents of the physical and vital bodies only reach to the level of the eyebrows, but the serpents of the astral, mental, causal, consciousness, and atmic bodies inevitably descend from the level of the eyebrows into the heart.

30. An accessory nerve goes from the spinal medulla into the heart. Through this accessory nerve our five superior serpents pass from the frontal region of the eyebrows into the heart.

31. This fine accessory thread of our spinal medulla controls the accessory muscles of the heart and has seven holy chambers.

32. There are seven holy centers within the heart. Each of our seven serpents is intimately related with a chamber of the heart.

33. Our disciples must have a system of purification and sanctification. The heart is the abode of our Innermost.

34. Disciples must make a list of all their defects. Then they must begin to amend them orderly and methodically.

35. The disciple could dedicate two months to amend each defect.

36. The hunter who wants to catch ten rabbits at one time will not catch a single one.

37. It is necessary to attain the most absolute sanctity and the most terrific chastity to acquire the development, progress, and evolution of the Kundalini.

38. Celibate (single) people should transmute their sexual energies with pranayama.

39. Married people (husband and wife) do not necessarily need to practice the breathing exercises, since pranayama is condensed for them in the practices of Sexual Magic.

40. It is only possible to practice Sexual Magic between husband and wife in legitimately constituted homes.

41. Whosoever practices Sexual Magic with different persons is an adulterer and a fornicator.

42. Revelation of Saint John calls this chakra the church of Thyatira.

43. *"I know thy works, and charity, and service, and faith, and thy patience (the necessary virtues that we must have in order to open the chakra of the heart), and thy works; and the last to be more than the first.*

    "Notwithstanding I have a few things against thee, because thou sufferest that woman Jezebel (fornication), which calleth herself a prophetess, to teach and to seduce my servants to commit fornication, and to eat things sacrificed unto idols (theories, intellectualism, that is to say, all kinds of meal offerings offered unto idols).

    "And I gave her space to repent of her fornication; and she repented not.

    "Behold, I will cast her into a bed, and them that commit adultery with her into great tribulation, except they repent of their deeds.

    "And I will kill her children with death; and all the churches shall know that I am he which searcheth the kidneys and hearts: and I will give unto every one of you according to your works."
    —Revelation 2:19-23

44. Above the kidneys there are two plexuses that in the chaste people irradiate blue and white colors, and in the fornicators a blood red color.

45. Our inner Christ searches the kidneys and hearts and gives unto each one of us what we deserve.

46. *"And he that overcometh, and keepeth my works (or commandments) unto the end, to him will I give power over the nations: Even as the power that I received of my Father I will give him the morning star."* —Revelation 2:26, 28

Vishuddha Chakra

THROAT

SANSKRIT NAME: VISHUDDHA

GREEK NAME: SARDIS

TIBETAN NAME: ENJOYMENT

DEVA / DEVATA: Sadashiva (Isvara Linga) and Shakini

POWERS: Comprehension, clairaudience, conceptual synthesis, scripture insight, knowledge of past, present, and future

REGION: Thyroid gland

SEED MANTRA: ह (ham)

TATTVA: Akash / Ether

VIRTUES REQUIRED: Upright speech, control of the tongue

VOWEL: E, pronounced "eh"

Chapter 9
The Chakra Vishuddha

1. The chakra Vishuddha of our spinal medulla is situated at the base of our creative larynx.

2. This marvelous chakra is intimately related with the Tattva Akash (ethereal element).

3. The color of this tattva is an intense blue.

4. The laryngeal chakra belongs to the Tattva Manas.

5. The divine deity that protects this marvelous chakra is Sadashiva.

6. This marvelous chakra has sixteen beautiful petals.

7. Indeed, the center of this chakra looks like a full moon.

8. The yogis from India affirm that by practicing meditation on this chakra, one is capable of sustaining one's living physical body even during the pralaya (cosmic night).

9. Whosoever learns to meditate on this chakra can know the highest esoteric knowledge of all the sacred books, including the Vedas.[101]

10. The yogi/yogini who learns to meditate on this chakra will reach the grand state of Trikala Jnani—that is to say, one who is capable of knowing the past, present, and future.

11. The mantra of the Tattva Akash is ह **Ham**. Undoubtedly, this mantra must be chanted by the yogi/yogini when meditating in this marvelous chakra.

12. *"And unto the angel of the church in Sardis write; These things saith he that hath the seven Spirits of God, and the seven stars; I know thy works, that thou hast a name that thou livest, and art dead.*

---

101 Sanskrit वेद् "knowledge," the oldest and most sacred scriptures of Hinduism.

13. *"Be watchful, and strengthen the things which remain, that are ready to die: for I have not found thy works perfect before God.*

14. *"Remember therefore how thou hast received and heard, and hold fast, and repent. If therefore thou shalt not watch, I will come on thee as a thief, and thou shalt not know what hour I will come upon thee.*

15. *"Thou hast a few names even in Sardis which have not defiled their garments; and they shall walk with me in white: for they are worthy.*

16. *"He that overcometh, the same shall be clothed in white raiment; and I will not blot out his name out of the book of life, but I will confess his name before my Father, and before his angels.*

17. *"He that hath an ear, let him hear what the Spirit saith unto the churches."* —Revelation 3:1-6

18. This chakra of the church of Sardis belongs to the sense of occult-hearing, clairaudience.

19. The mental body is intimately related with the church of Sardis.

20. I, Samael Aun Weor, planetary Logos of Mars, after many mahamanvantaras of incessant evolution and progress, have arrived at the conclusion that the only essential thing in life is sanctity.

21. Powers [siddhis] are flowers of the soul that sprout when we have sanctified ourselves.

22. For one step that we take in the development of the chakras, we must take a thousand steps in sanctity.

23. We prepare our garden with the esoteric exercises so that we can make our marvelous chakras bloom with the perfume of sanctity.

24. The yogi/yogini must water one's garden daily by finishing with all of one's moral defects.

25. Each petal of our lotus flowers represents certain virtues; without these virtues, the lotus flowers cannot open to receive the sun of truth.

26. Do not covet powers, because you will sink into the lunar abysses.

27. It is better for those who do not want to sanctify themselves to withdraw from these teachings before it is too late for them.

28. The Vishuddha chakra is related with the creative word.

29. Sometimes to speak is a crime, and sometimes to be silent is a crime.

30. There are delinquent silences, and words of infamy.

31. The most difficult thing in life is to learn how to control our tongue.

Ajna Chakra

FRONTAL

SANSKRIT NAME: AJNA

GREEK NAME: PHILADELPHIA

TIBETAN NAME: WHITE CONCH

DEVA / DEVATA: Paramashiva
  and Hakini (Shakti)

POWERS: Clairvoyance

REGION: Pituitary gland

SEED MANTRA: ॐ (om)

TATTVA: Adi / Light

VIRTUES REQUIRED: Serenity

VOWEL: I, pronounced "ee"

Chapter 10
The Chakra Ajna

1. This chakra is connected to its marvelous center located between the eyebrows.
2. The master who directs this center is Paramashiva.
3. The mantra that makes this chakra vibrate is ॐ **Om:** *Ooooooooommmmmmmmmm.*
4. This chakra has two petals.
5. This marvelous chakra has a very pure white color. The cavernous plexus corresponds to this chakra.
6. The yogis from India state that by meditating on this chakra one can destroy the karmas of past lives.
7. I, Samael, Logos of Mars, state that nobody can mock the law.
8. The best that we can do is to learn how to handle our negotiations.
9. Whosoever has capital can pay one's debts and do well in one's negotiations.
10. Perform good deeds so that you may pay your debts.
11. The lion of the law is fought with the scale.
12. When an inferior law is transcended by a superior law, the superior law washes away the inferior law.
13. The yogi/yogini must learn how to travel in one's astral body so that one can visit the Temple of Anubis and his 42 judges.
14. In the temple of the lords of karma we can arrange our negotiations (karmic debts).
15. We can also ask for credit from the lords of karma, but every credit must be paid by working in the Great Work of the Father, or by suffering the unspeakable.
16. The chakra Ajna is the chakra of clairvoyance, psychic vision.

17.   The plexus of this chakra is a lotus flower that sprouts from the pituitary gland. This gland is the page or light bearer of the pineal gland, where the crown of the saints, the lotus of one thousand petals, the eye of Dangma, the eye of intuition, is situated.

18.   Psychic clairvoyance by itself, without the development of the coronary chakra, could lead the yogi/yogini astray into grave errors.

19.   There are billions of black magicians in the astral and mental planes; they disguise themselves as saints or masters of the White Lodge to mislead the disciples or to dictate false oracles to them.

20.   The only way to avoid those possible errors is by awakening intuition, whose divine diamond eye is in the lotus of a thousand petals that we are going to study in the next chapter.

21.   The yogi/yogini who wants to project oneself in the astral body must take advantage of that transition state between vigil and sleep.

22.   The yogi/yogini shall get up out of one's bed in the very instant of falling asleep and go out of one's bedroom towards the palace of the lords of karma to arrange one's negotiations. One can go to any temple of mysteries.

23.   This former procedure must be executed with actions; it is not a mere mental exercise.

24.   The yogi/yogini must get up from their bed in the instants of getting sleepy, just as a sleepwalker does.

25.   Triumph is attained with patience and perseverance.

26.   In former chapters, we have taught the mantras and the practices for the chakras of the spinal column.

27.   However, we must not forget that the plexuses also have mantras.

28.   The powerful Egyptian mantra **Fe Unin Dagj** makes all of our plexuses vibrate. What is important is to prolong the sound of the vowels.

29. The vowels I, E, O, U, A are arranged in the following order:

> I: frontal plexus
>
> E: larynx plexus
>
> O: cardiac plexus
>
> U: solar plexus
>
> A: plexus of the lungs

30. We can awaken all of our hidden powers by meditating on each of these vowels, making the sound travel from between the eyebrows down to the throat, and then to the heart, the solar plexus, the legs, and finally to the feet.

31. Whosoever learns how to meditate on the Ajna chakra will acquire the eight major siddhis and the lesser thirty-two.

32. This is the church of Philadelphia.

> *"I know thy works: behold, I have set before thee an open door, and no man can shut it: for thou hast a little strength, and hast kept my word, and hast not denied my name.*

33. *"Behold, I will make them of the synagogue of Satan, which say they are Jews, and are not, but do lie; behold, I will make them to come and worship before thy feet, and to know that I have loved thee.*

34. *"Because thou hast kept the word of my patience, I also will keep thee from the hour of temptation, which shall come upon all the world, to try them that dwell upon the earth."* —Revelation 3:8-10

35. In the mental and astral planes, we are tempted by billions of demons. Many of these demons disguise themselves as saints and masters to tempt and deceive us.

36. Psychic clairvoyance is set as an open door before you; however, it is necessary for you to acquire strength and to keep the word of God so as to not fall into temptation.

37. *"Because thou hast kept the word of my patience, I also will keep thee from the hour of temptation, which shall come upon all the world, to try them that dwell upon the earth."* —Revelation 3:10

38. In the Mental Plane there are black magicians who very cunningly advise us to perform seminal ejaculation.

39. Those black magicians disguise themselves as saints and pronounce sublime speeches of love and sanctity.

40. *"Behold, I come quickly: hold that fast which thou hast, that no man take thy crown."* —Revelation 3:11

41. Those tenebrous entities advise the student to ejaculate his seminal fluid, to make his seminal liquor descend, thus taking away his crown.

42. *"Him that overcometh will I make a pillar in the temple of my God, and he shall go no more out: and I will write upon him the name of my God, and the name of the city of my God, which is new Jerusalem, which cometh down out of heaven from my God: and I will write upon him my new name.*

43. *"He that hath an ear, let him hear what the Spirit saith unto the churches."* —Revelation 3:12-13

Chapter 11

The Chakra Sahasrara

1. The chakra Sahasrara is the crown of saints. It is the abode of Lord Shiva and corresponds to the pineal gland.

2. The crown of saints is attained when Devi Kundalini reaches this chakra.

3. The crown of saints has twelve stars.

4. These twelve stars are twelve faculties in the true human being.

5. There are twenty-four angelic atoms in the brain; these atoms represent the twenty-four elders of the zodiac.

Sahasrara

6. The twenty-four atomic elders of our brain ardently shine when Devi Kundalini opens the marvelous chakra.

7. This center has a thousand petals. This is the church of Laodicea.

8. The Revelation of Saint John warns us:

   "I know thy works, that thou art neither cold nor hot: I would thou wert cold or hot.

   So then because thou art lukewarm, and neither cold nor hot, I will spew thee out of my mouth." —Revelation 3:15-16

9. Indeed, lukewarm souls are cast out of the temple of wisdom.

10. This wisdom is for ardent souls.

11. The twenty-four atomic elders represent the entire wisdom of the twenty-four elders of the zodiac.

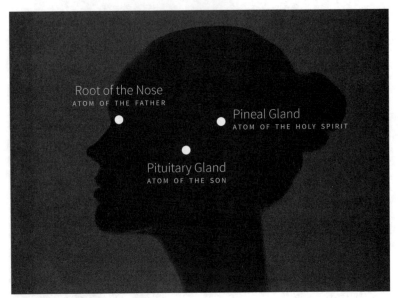

Three Atoms

12. The twenty-four zodiacal elders dressed in white garments are seated on the throne of our brain.

13. The atom[102] of the Father is situated in the root of our nose.

14. This is the atom of willpower.

15. Through dominating the animal impulse by willpower the seven serpents of our seven bodies rise.

16. The atom of the Son abides in the pituitary gland, whose exponent is the Nous Atom[103] (the Son of Man) in the heart.

17. The atomic angel of the Holy Spirit shines within the chakra Sahasrara in the pineal gland.

---

102 Atoms are "Minute bodies of intelligence possessing the dual attributes of Nature and man." While there are many types and levels of such atomic intelligences, both positive and negative, some of particular importance are Aspiring atoms, Destructive atoms, the Nous atom, Informer atoms, Scholar atoms, etc. Read *The Dayspring of Youth* by M.

103 A spiritual atom located in the left ventricle of the heart. This atom is also called the Master Atom and is directly related with the Christ.

18. The atom of the Father controls the magnetic ganglionic cord of the right, Pingala.

19. The atom of the Son governs the canal of Sushumna.

20. The atom of the Holy Spirit governs Ida.

21. This is why the atom of the Holy Spirit is intimately related with our sexual energies and with the rays of the Moon, which are related with human reproduction.

22. *"Behold, I stand at the door, and knock: if any man hears my voice, and opens the door, I will come in to him, and will sup with him, and he with me."* —Revelation 3:20

23. This is the wedding feast of the Lamb with the Soul.

24. When we have raised the seven serpents of fire upon the staff, He stands at the door and knocks.

25. He then comes into his temple.

26. Then He sups with us and we with Him.

27. *"To him that overcometh, will I grant to sit with me in my throne; even as I also overcame and am set down with my Father in his throne."* —Revelation: 3:21

28. This is the great event of Bethlehem; this is the Nativity of the heart.

29. This is the descent of Christ into the atomic infernos of the human being.

30. *"And there appeared a great wonder in heaven; a woman clothed with the sun, and the moon under her feet, and upon her head a crown of twelve stars."* —Revelation 12:1

31. This woman dressed with the Sun is the Christified Soul.

32. *"And she being with child cried, travailing in birth, and pained to be delivered."* —Revelation 12: 2

33. *"And she brought forth a man child, who was to rule all nations with a rod of iron: and her child was caught up unto God, and to his throne."* —Revelation 12:5

34. That man-child is our inner Christ in gestation, that finally is born in us, and transforms us into Christs.

Sahasrara Chakra

CROWN
SANSKRIT NAME: SAHASRARA
GREEK NAME: LAODICEA
TIBETAN NAME: GREAT BLISS

DEVA / DEVATA: Shiva

POWERS: Polyvoyance, intuition, multidimensional travel

REGION: Pineal gland

TATTVA: Samadhi

VIRTUES REQUIRED: Devotion, sanctity, willpower

VOWEL: I, pronounced "ee"

35. When Jesus received the baptism in the Jordan, John told him, "Jesus, you have received the Christ. Now you are a Christ."

36. There are 144,000 angelic atoms within our brain. Those angelic atoms govern all the atoms in our human organism.

37. The pituitary gland, or sixth sense, is the page, the light-bearer of the pineal gland where the crown of the saints is situated.

38. The internal reconcentration is more important than clairvoyance.

39. Clairvoyance is useful in all planes of consciousness.

40. Nevertheless, in the inferior planes the tenebrous entities can lead the seers astray.

41. The demons disguise themselves as angels.

42. Whosoever advises seminal ejaculation [orgasm] is a black magician.

43. We open the diamond eye (the pineal gland) by means of internal reconcentration; thus, we enter into the superior worlds of fire where the truth reigns.

44. The clairvoyant who does not awaken intuition could become a slanderer of a neighbor, and even an assassin.

45. Intuition allow us to know the internal reality of all the images that float in the Astral Light.[104] The intuitive clairvoyant is omniscient.

46. A clairvoyant without intuition is like a ship without a compass or a ship without a steering wheel. The intuitive clairvoyant is powerful.

47. Each of the seven chakras of the spinal column is governed by an atomic angel.

48. *"And I saw another mighty angel come down from heaven, clothed with a cloud: and a rainbow was upon his head, and his face was as it were the sun, and his feet as pillars of fire."*
—Revelation 10:1

104 See glossary.

49. That mighty angel is our Innermost, crowned with a heavenly rainbow, the chakra Sahasrara of the pineal gland, whose resplendency is terribly divine.

50. *"And cried with a loud voice, as when a lion roareth: and when he had cried, seven thunders uttered their voices."*
—Revelation 10:3

51. These seven thunders are the seven notes of the Lost Word that resound in the seven churches of our spinal medulla.

52. Each of the seven angels of the seven churches sound their trumpet; they sound their key note as the sacred fire of Devi Kundalini ascends throughout the Brahmanadi of our Sushumna canal.

53. *"But in the days of the voice of the seventh angel (the atomic angel of the Sahasrara chakra) when he shall begin to sound the trumpet (which is his secret note), the mystery of God shall be consummated, as He hath declared to his servants the Prophets."*
—Revelation 10:7

54. The mantra **Aum** serves to open the chakras of the grand sympathetic nervous system.

55. **Auim** for the cavernous plexus of the pituitary gland, the center of clairvoyance.

56. **Auem** for the plexus of the thyroid gland, the center of clairaudience.

57. **Auom** for the heart, the center of intuition.

58. **Aum** for the solar plexus, region of the epigastria, the telepathic center.

59. **Auam** for the chakra of the lungs that allows us to remember our past lives.

60. **Aum** is a proto-tattvic mantra that allows us to awaken our Tattvic powers. To chant it open the mouth with the vowel A, round it with the vowel U and close it with the M.

    Apply the same system for all the other mantras: **Auim, Auem, Auom, Aum, Auam.**

Chapter 12
The Seven Seals

1. When we have formed our inner Christ, He then enters into all of our vehicles through the pineal gland.

2. The inner Christ has the shape of a small child. He comes out of his ethereal womb to enter into our physical body through the pineal gland.

3. This is the descent of Christ into the atomic infernos of the human being.

4. This is the Nativity of the heart.

5. It is how we transform ourselves into Christs.

6. Nature does not leap; this is why our inner Christ is born within us as a small child.

7. The three wise men (the Malachim) adore him and offer him gold, incense, and myrrh.

8. These three King Magi are the Innermost, the Divine Soul, and the Human Soul (Atman-Buddhi-Manas).

9. The Star of Bethlehem is the Central Sun; it is the universal Great Breath of life.

10. Our inner Christ is only one particle of the spiritual Central Sun.

11. The entire universe of Pleroma,[105] the whole thought of God, is reflected within our inner Christ.

12. Our inner Christ is the Word.

13. With the event of Bethlehem, the Word becomes flesh within our heart.

14. We must clearly distinguish between the seven churches and the seven seals mentioned in Revelation.

---

105 Greek πλήρωμα "fullness," an ancient Gnostic term for the divine world or universal soul. Space, developed and divided into a series of aeons. The abode of the invisible gods. In correspondence to the Kabbalah, Pleroma refers to the world of Atziluth.

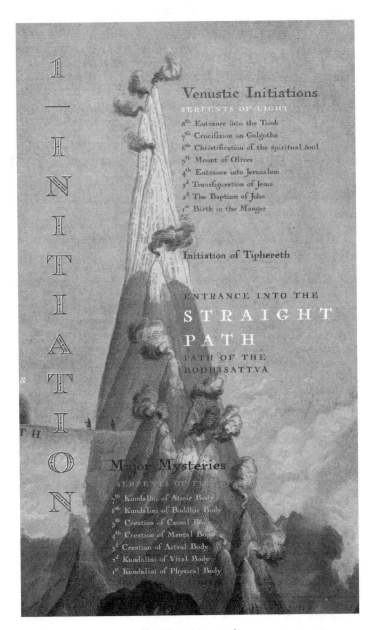

The First Mountain

The Seven Seals are the Venustic Initiations (top), and occur after the Serpents of Fire (Major Mysteries) and the entrance into the straight path. Read The Three Mountains by Samael Aun Weor.

15. The seven churches are related to the seven chakras of our spinal column.

16. The seven seals are the seven white spiritual serpents of our inner Christ.[106]

17. These seven serpents are the spiritual part of the seven columns of fire of Devi Kundalini.

18. The seven serpents of our inner Christ are no longer fiery, but rather they are beyond fire, even though they are the cause of fire.

19. These are the seven seals of the Revelation of St. John.

20. These seven seals can be opened only by the Lamb, our inner Christ.

21. *"And I saw in the right hand of him that sat on the throne a book written within and on the backside, sealed with seven seals.*

22. *"And I saw a strong angel proclaiming with a loud voice, who is worthy to open the book, and to loose the seals thereof?*

23. *"And no man in heaven, nor in earth, neither under the earth, was able to open the book, neither to look thereon."*
    —Revelation 5:1-3

24. The book is the human being, and the seven seals are the seven spiritual serpents of our Inner Christ.

25. These serpents can be raised only by the Lamb.

26. *"And I saw when the Lamb opened one of the Seals, and I heard as it were the voice of thunder, one of the four beasts saying: Come and see."* —Revelation 6:1

27. When the Lamb opens the first seal, the white horse appears as the symbol of the physical body.

28. When the Lamb opens the second seal, the red horse appears as the symbol of the ethereal body.

29. When the Lamb opens the third seal, the black horse appears as the symbol of the body of desires (astral body).

---

106 Also called Venustic Initiations. "These seven Serpents of Light are the Seven Seals of Apocalypse (Revelation), which only the Lamb, the 'I Am,' can open." —Samael Aun Weor

30. When the Lamb opens the fourth seal, the wisdom of the great Illuminati is granted to us. This occurs when the inner Christ takes complete possession of the mental body of the human being. This is the yellow horse.

31. When the Lamb opens the fifth seal, the human souls appear dressed in white garments.

32. When the Lamb opens the sixth seal, the sun becomes dark like black cloth and the moon becomes as blood. Then we are stricken with great pain, because the consciousness only awakens through pain and bitterness.

33. Finally, when the Lamb opens the seventh seal, the seven atomic angels of our organism sound their trumpets in triumph, announcing victory.

34. *"And when he had opened the seventh seal, there was silence in heaven about the space of half an hour."* —Revelation 8:1

35. This is how the Child-God of Bethlehem grows within us.

36. The Child-God of Bethlehem has to be absorbed within all of his bodhisattva.[107] He performs this by raising his seven spiritual serpents.

37. So, when finally the Child-God of Bethlehem is absorbed within his bodhisattva, he tosses his bodhisattva back into the inner depths of the consciousness. This is how the Child-God comes from within to without, to the world of the flesh, to lean out through the five senses and to appear as a Christ among mankind, and thus to perform the work of the Father.

38. Do not confuse the seven igneous serpents of the soul with the seven totally Christic and spiritual serpents of the inner Christ.

39. The four horses of the Apocalypse are our four bodies of sin,[108] the four gross bodies that constitute our inferior personality.

40. The Lamb has to raise each one of these Christic serpents in successive order; first one, then the other, and so on.

---

107 A human soul who has incarnated Christ. See glossary.
108 Physical, vital, astral, and mental bodies.

41. This work is very arduous and difficult.

42. The horseman on the white horse triumphs with his bow and arrow. Thus the physical world is dominated. The horseman on the red horse has the power to take peace away, and also to give peace, because the ethereal body is the base of the physical body.

43. The horseman on the black horse has to vanquish the weight of desire, lust, greed, and all the lower passions.

44. The name of the horseman of the yellow horse is Death; and hell and death follow him because the mental body is constituted by the atomic infernos of the human being, where death reigns.

45. Everything within the human mind belongs to desire. Therefore, they have to die.

46. All the thought-rubbish must fall dead before the temple door.[109] This is why the name of the fourth horseman is Death. And all the bitterness from hell follows him.

47. The Earth is the twin sister of Venus.

48. All the events that happen on Venus are repeated on Earth.

49. The light of the Sun reaches Earth through Venus.

50. Venus receives three times more solar light than the Earth.

51. Venus is the solar light bearer.

52. The Genie of the Earth has to receive instructions from the Genie of Venus.

53. Uriel, the Genie of Venus, is the Master of Cham-Gam,[110] the Genie of the Earth.

54. If the light of the Sun comes to Earth through Venus, then we have no other choice than to appeal to Venus in order to be able to reach the Solar Logos.

109 "... the shrine must of all action, sound, or earthly light be void; e'en as the butterfly, o'ertaken by the frost, falls lifeless at the threshold — so must all earthly thoughts fall dead before the fane." —*Voice of the Silence*
110 Melchizedek

55. Venus is Love.

56. The Kundalini develops and progresses by means of Sexual Magic.

57. God shines on the perfect couple.

58. Sexual Magic was practiced in the Eleusinian mysteries,[111] along with the holy dances and naked dances to awaken and develop Devi Kundalini.

59. In the stone courtyards of the Aztec temples, young men and women remained sexually connected, loving each other for months in order to awaken Devi Kundalini.

60. There is no greater joy than love.

61. The only way men and women can transform themselves into gods is by adoring each other. Any other way is a waste of time.

62. Venus is the first star that shines before the sunrise.

63. Venus is the first star that shines when the sun sets.

64. Venus is the Light-bearer.

65. Venus is love.

66. God shines on the beings who love each other.

---

111 Greek religious tradition.

Chapter 13

Internal Meditation

1. Internal meditation is a scientific system to receive information.

2. The wise submerges into meditation to search for information.

3. Meditation is the daily bread of the wise.

4. Meditation has different steps.

    a. Asana: posture of the body

    b. Pratyahara: serene mind

    c. Dharana: internal concentration

    d. Dhyana: internal meditation

    e. Samadhi: ecstasy

5. Firstly, we must place our body in a very comfortable position.

6. Before starting our concentration we have to place our mind in serenity; that is to say, we have to remove every type of thought from our mind.

7. After having accomplished the former steps, we then rise up to the steps of dharana, dhyana, and samadhi.

8. Whosoever follows the path of Jnana Yoga[112] converts oneself into a sannyasin[113] of thought.

9. First, we concentrate our mind on the physical body; then after meditating profoundly about the nature of this marvelous vehicle, we discard it from the mind by saying, "I am not the physical body."

10. Then, we concentrate our thought on our ethereal body, and we discard it by saying, "I am not the ethereal body."

11. Then after, we meditate on the astral and mental bodies.

---

112 Sanskrit, from the root jna, "to know."

113 Sanskrit संन्यासिन्, literally "who has cast aside, one who abandons or resigns worldly affairs, devotee" a renunciate.

12. The astral and mental bodies are the two columns of the temple that rest upon the cubic stone of Yesod. That cubic stone is the ethereal body. The disciple has to pass between those two columns of the temple.

13. Those two columns are Jachin and Boaz—one black and the other white.[114]

14. The word INRI is written with characters of fire upon those columns.

15. This word INRI is a password that allows us to pass between the two columns of the temple to function without material vehicles of any type within the World of the Mist of Fire.

16. The disciple will meditate profoundly on these two columns, which are the astral and mental bodies. The disciple will relax profoundly while mentally chanting the mantra INRI, prolonging the sound of each letter by imitating the sharp sound of the crickets of the forest, thus, until achieving that sound, until giving unto the letters that sharp sound, a sound synthesis like a prolonged "S," as follows: Sssssssssssssssssssssssssssssssssss......

17. It is necessary to identify oneself with that sibilant very sharp sound, similar to the most elevated note that a fine flute can give.

18. In the august Rome of the Caesars, the cricket was considered sacred and was sold in golden cages at very high prices.

19. If we can have that little creature close to our ears and meditate profoundly on its sound, then the sharp note that the cricket emits would awaken the same sound in our brain.

20. Then we could rise from our bed with our astral body and with complete consciousness travel towards the Gnostic Church.

---

114 Hebrew, two symbolic pillars of the Temple of Solomon, the solar human; the astral solar body and the mental solar body (Hod and Netzach).

21. That is the subtle voice mentioned by Apollonius of Tyana. That is the still small voice that Elijah heard in the entrance in of the cave.

22. Let us read some verses of the Bible:

    "And he said, Go forth, and stand upon the mount before the LORD. And, behold, the LORD passed by, and a great and strong wind rent the mountains, and brake in pieces the rocks before the LORD; but the LORD was not in the wind: and after the wind an earthquake; but the LORD was not in the earthquake:

23. *"And after the earthquake a fire; but the LORD was not in the fire: and after the fire a still small voice.*

24. *"And it was so, when Elijah heard it that he wrapped his face in his mantle, and went out, and stood in the entrance of the cave.*

    And, behold, there came a voice unto him, and said, What doest thou here, Elijah?" —1 Kings 19:11-13

25. The deeply relaxed disciple will meditate profoundly on the black column (the astral body) and will try to hear the still, small voice, while saying, "I am not the astral body."

26. The disciple will then meditate profoundly on the white column (the mental body) and will try to hear the still small voice, the subtle voice, the essence of INRI, the sibilant "S," the sharp sound of the crickets from the forests; thus, while becoming profoundly drowsy, one will discard the mental body by saying, "I am not the mental body."

27. Now, the disciple will concentrate one's entire mind on one's willpower, and will discard the body of willpower by saying, "I am not willpower either."

28. Now let the disciple concentrate one's mind on one's consciousness, on Buddhi (body of the consciousness) and discard oneself from that marvelous body by saying, "I am not the consciousness either."

29. Now let the disciple concentrate oneself in the Innermost, become profoundly drowsy, take a totally

childlike attitude, and say, "I am the Innermost. I am the Innermost. I am the Innermost."

30. Let the disciple become even more drowsy and say, "The Innermost is just the child of the inner Christ."

31. Let the disciple profoundly meditate on the inner Christ.

32. Now the disciple should be absorbed within the inner Christ. Let the disciple be absorbed in Him, in Him, in Him.

33. Let the disciple say to oneself, "I am He. I am He. I am He."

34. The mantra **Pander** allows us to identify ourselves with our Inner Christ, so to act as Christ within the universe of Pleroma.

35. May the disciple become profoundly drowsy, because drowsiness is the bridge that allows us to pass from meditation into samadhi.[115]

36. There are many types of samadhi: astral samadhi, mental samadhi, causal samadhi, samadhi within the consciousness, samadhi within the Innermost, and samadhi within the inner Christ.

37. In the first samadhi, we only enter into the astral plane. In the second type of samadhi, we soar with the mental body throughout space.

38. In the third type of samadhi, we function within the world of willpower without material vehicles of any type. In the fourth type of samadhi, we soar with the Buddhic body throughout space.

---

115 "Meditation must be combined intelligently with concentration and drowsiness. Concentration mixed with drowsiness produces enlightenment. Many esotericists think that meditation in no way should be combined with the drowsiness of the body, but those who think that way are wrong, because meditation without drowsiness ruins the brain. Always use sleep in combination with the technique of meditation, but a controlled sleep... We must "ride" on sleep, and not let the sleep ride on us." —Samael Aun Weor, The Conquest of the Illuminating Void "Drowsiness in combination with meditation produces ecstasy." —Samael Aun Weor, The Aquarian Message

39. In the fifth type of samadhi, we can move in the Innermost without vehicles of any type throughout the World of the Mist of Fire.

40. With the sixth type of samadhi, we can function in the inner Christ.

41. There is a seventh type of samadhi for the great masters of samadhi. In this samadhi, we can visit the nucleoli upon which the entire universe is based. Those nucleoli, speaking in an allegorical way, are openings through which we can observe the terrific majesty of the Absolute.

May the peace of the Father be with ye.

Glossary

Absolute: Abstract space; that which is without attributes or limitations. Also known as sunyata, void, emptiness, Parabrahman, Adi-buddha, and many other names.

"The Absolute is the Being of all Beings. The Absolute is that which Is, which always has Been, and which always will Be. The Absolute is expressed as Absolute Abstract Movement and Repose. The Absolute is the cause of Spirit and of Matter, but It is neither Spirit nor Matter. The Absolute is beyond the mind; the mind cannot understand It. Therefore, we have to intuitively understand Its nature." —Samael Aun Weor, *Tarot and Kabbalah*

"In the Absolute we go beyond karma and the gods, beyond the law. The mind and the individual consciousness are only good for mortifying our lives. In the Absolute we do not have an individual mind or individual consciousness; there, we are the unconditioned, free and absolutely happy Being. The Absolute is life free in its movement, without conditions, limitless, without the mortifying fear of the law, life beyond spirit and matter, beyond karma and suffering, beyond thought, word and action, beyond silence and sound, beyond forms." —Samael Aun Weor, *The Major Mysteries*

Aquarius: An era of time under the influence of the zodiacal sign of Aquarius that will last for approximately 2,140 years. The new Aquarian era began with the celestial conjunction of February 4-5, 1962. On February 4-5, 1962, exactly when there was a new moon AND a full solar eclipse, there was also an extraordinary celestial conjunction of the seven primary planets with the Earth. The Sun, the Moon, Mercury, Venus, Mars, Jupiter, and Saturn were all visibly grouped close together, and their orbits were aligned with the Earth. This event signaled a change of era, similar to how the hands of a clock move into a new day. The Earth had completed an era of approximately 2,140 years under the influence of Pisces, and then entered an era influenced by Aquarius.

When the age of Aquarius arrived, humanity entered into a very new situation. With the new celestial influence we saw the arrival of a huge shift in society: mass rebellion against the old ways, sexual experimentation, giant social earthquakes shaking up all the old traditions. We also saw the arrival in the West of a strong spiritual longing, and deep thirst for true, authentic spiritual experience. These two elements: 1) rebellion to tradition and 2) thirst for spiritual knowledge are a direct effect of the influence of Aquarius, the most revolutionary sign of the zodiac. Aquarius is the Water Carrier, whose occult significance is knowledge, the bringer of knowledge. With the new age came a sudden revealing of all the hidden knowledge. The doors to the mysteries were thrown open so that humanity can save itself from itself. Of course, the Black Lodge, ever-eager to mislead humanity, has produced so much false spirituality and so many false schools that it is very difficult to find the real and genuine path.

"The majority of the tenebrous brothers and sisters of Aquarius are wicked people who are going around teaching black magic." —Samael Aun Weor, *The Major Mysteries*

"The age of sex, the new Aquarian Age, is at hand. The sexual glands are controlled by the planet Uranus which is the ruling planet of the constellation of Aquarius. Thus, sexual alchemy is in fact the science of the new Aquarian Age. Sexual Magic will be officially accepted in the universities of the new Aquarian Age. Those who presume to be messengers of the new Aquarian Age, but nevertheless hate the Arcanum A.Z.F., provide more than enough evidence that they are truly impostors, this is because the new Aquarian Age is governed by the regent of sex. This regent is the planet Uranus. Sexual energy is the finest energy of the infinite cosmos. Sexual energy can convert us into angels or demons. The image of truth is found deposited in sexual energy. The cosmic design of Adam Christ is found deposited in sexual energy." —Samael Aun Weor, *The Perfect Matrimony*

To learn more about the Aquarian era, read *Christ and the Virgin* by Samael Aun Weor.

Arcanum: (Latin. plural: arcana). A secret, a mystery. The root of the term "ark" as in the Ark of Noah and the Ark of the Covenent.

Arcanum A.Z.F.: The practice of sexual transmutation as couple (male-female), a technique known in Tantra and Alchemy. Arcanum refers to a hidden truth or law. A.Z.F. stands for A (agua, water), Z (azufre, sulfur), F (fuego, fire), and is thus: water + fire = consciousness. . Also, A (azoth = chemical element that refers to fire). A & Z are the first and last letters of the alphabet thus referring to the Alpha & Omega (beginning & end).

Aryan Race: "(Sanskrit) arya [from the verbal root to rise, tend upward] Holy, hallowed, highly evolved or especially trained; a title of the Hindu rishis [initiates]. Originally a term of ethical as well as intellectual and spiritual excellence, belonging to those who had completely mastered the aryasatyani (holy truths) and who had entered upon the aryamarga (path leading to moksha or nirvana). It was originally applicable only to the initiates or adepts of the ancient Aryan peoples, but today Aryan has become the name of a race of the human family in its various branches. All ancient peoples had their own term for initiates or adepts, as for instance among the ancient Hebrews the generic name Israel, or Sons of Israel." —Theosophical Glossary

"From Sanskrit [=a]rya excellent, honorable; akin to the name of the country Iran, and perh. to Erin, Ireland, and the early name of this people, at least in Asia. 1. One of a primitive people supposed to have lived in prehistoric times, in Central Asia, east of the Caspian Sea, and north of the Hindoo Koosh and Paropamisan Mountains, and to have been the stock from which sprang the Hindoo, Persian, Greek, Latin, Celtic, Teutonic, Slavonic, and other races; one of that ethnological division of mankind called also Indo-European or Indo-Germanic." —Webster's Revised Unabridged Dictionary

While formerly it was believed that the ancient Aryans were European (white), most scientists now believe that the ancient people commonly referred to as Aryan were the original inhabitants of India, which Manu called Aryavarta, "Abode of the Aryans." However, in universal Gnosticism, the word Aryan refers not to "white people" or to an ancient, dead civilization, but instead refers to to the vast majority of the population of this planet. In Gnosis, all modern races are "Aryan."

Astral Body: What is commonly called the astral body is not the true astral body, it is rather the lunar protoplasmatic body, also known as the kama rupa (Sanskrit, "body of desires") or "dream body" (Tibetan rmi-lam-gyi lus). The true astral body is solar (being superior to lunar nature) and must be created, as the Master Jesus indicated in the Gospel of John 3:5-6, "Except a man be born of water and of the Spirit, he cannot enter into the kingdom of God. That which is born of the flesh is flesh; and that which is born of the Spirit is spirit." The solar astral body is created as a result of the Third Initiation of Major Mysteries (Serpents of Fire), and is perfected in the Third Serpent of Light. In Tibetan Buddhism, the solar astral body is known as the illusory body (sgyu-lus). This body is related to the emotional center and to the sephirah Hod.

"Really, only those who have worked with the Maithuna (White Tantra) for many years can possess the astral body." —Samael Aun Weor, *The Elimination of Satan's Tail*

Astral Light: "There has been an infinite confusion of names to express one and the same thing. The chaos of the ancients; the Zoroastrian sacred fire, or the Antusbyrum of the Parsees; the Hermes-fire; the Elmes-fire of the ancient Germans; the lightning of Cybele; the burning torch of Apollo; the flame on the altar of Pan; the inextinguishable fire in the temple on the Acropolis, and in that of Vesta; the fire-flame of Pluto's helm; the brilliant sparks on the hats of the Dioscuri, on the Gorgon head, the helm of Pallas, and the staff of Mercury; the πυρ ασβεστον the Egyptian Phtha, or Ra; the Grecian Zeus Cataibates (the descending); the pentecostal fire-tongues; the burning bush of Moses; the pillar of fire of the Exodus, and the "burning lamp" of Abram; the eternal fire of the "bottomless pit"; the Delphic oracular vapors; the Sidereal light of the Rosicrucians; the AKASA of the Hindu adepts; the Astral light of Eliphas Levi; the nerve-aura and the fluid of the magnetists; the od of Reichenbach; the fire-globe, or meteor-cat of Babinet; the Psychod and ectenic force of Thury; the psychic force of Sergeant Cox and Mr. Crookes; the atmospheric magnetism of some naturalists; galvanism; and finally, electricity, are but various names for many different manifestations, or effects of the same mysterious, all-pervading cause--the Greek Archeus, or Αρχαιοσ. [...] The thaumaturgists of all periods, schools, and countries,

produced their wonders, because they were perfectly familiar with the im-
ponderable--in their effects--but otherwise perfectly tangible waves of the
astral light. They controlled the currents by guiding them with their willpower. The wonders were both of physical and psychological character;
the former embracing effects produced upon material objects, the latter
the mental phenomena of Mesmer and his successors. This class has been
represented in our time by two illustrious men, Du Potet and Regazzoni,
whose wonderful powers were well attested in France and other countries.
Mesmerism is the most important branch of magic; and its phenomena
are the effects of the universal agent which underlies all magic and has
produced at all ages the so-called miracles. The ancients called it Chaos;
Plato and the Pythagoreans named it the Soul of the World. According
to the Hindus, the Deity in the shape of Æther pervades all things. It is
the invisible, but, as we have said before, too tangible Fluid. Among other
names this universal Proteus--or "the nebulous Almighty," as de Mirville
calls it in derision--was termed by the theurgists "the living fire," the
"Spirit of Light," and Magnes. This last appellation indicates its magnetic
properties and shows its magical nature. For, as truly expressed by one of
its enemies--μάγος and μάγνες are two branches growing from the same
trunk, and shooting forth the same resultants. Magnetism is a word for
the derivation of which we have to look to an incredibly early epoch. The
stone called magnet is believed by many to owe its name to Magnesia, a
city or district in Thessaly, where these stones were found in quantity. We
believe, however, the opinion of the Hermetists to be the correct one. The
word Magh, magus, is derived from the Sanskrit Mahaji, the great or wise
(the anointed by the divine wisdom). [...] Now, what is this mystic, primordial substance? In the book of Genesis, at the beginning of the first
chapter, it is termed the "face of the waters," said to have been incubated
by the "Spirit of God." Job mentions, in chap. xxvi., 5, that "dead things
are formed from under the waters, and inhabitants thereof." In the
original text, instead of "dead things," it is written dead Rephaim (giants,
or mighty primitive men), from whom "Evolution" may one day trace our
present race. In the Egyptian mythology, Kneph the Eternal unrevealed
God is represented by a snake-emblem of eternity encircling a water-
urn, with his head hovering over the waters, which it incubates with his
breath. In this case the serpent is the Agathodaimon, the good spirit; in
its opposite aspect it is the Kakodaimon--the bad one. In the Scandina-
vian Eddas, the honey-dew--the food of the gods and of the creative, busy
Yggdrasill--bees--falls during the hours of night, when the atmosphere
is impregnated with humidity; and in the Northern mythologies, as the
passive principle of creation, it typifies the creation of the universe out
of water; this dew is the astral light in one of its combinations and possesses creative as well as destructive properties. In the Chaldean legend of
Berosus, Oannes or Dagon, the man-fish, instructing the people, shows
the infant world created out of water and all beings originating from
this prima materia. Moses teaches that only earth and water can bring a
living soul; and we read in the Scriptures that herbs could not grow until

the Eternal caused it to rain upon earth. In the Mexican Popol-Vuh man is created out of mud or clay (terre glaise), taken from under the water. Brahma creates Lomus, the great Muni (or first man), seated on his lotus, only after having called into being, spirits, who thus enjoyed among mortals a priority of existence, and he creates him out of water, air, and earth. Alchemists claim that primordial or pre-Adamic earth when reduced to its first substance is in its second stage of transformation like clear-water, the first being the alkahest proper. This primordial substance is said to contain within itself the essence of all that goes to make up man; it has not only all the elements of his physical being, but even the "breath of life" itself in a latent state, ready to be awakened. This it derives from the "incubation" of the Spirit of God upon the face of the waters--chaos; in fact, this substance is chaos itself. From this it was that Paracelsus claimed to be able to make his "homunculi"; and this is why Thales, the great natural philosopher, maintained that water was the principle of all things in nature. What is the primordial Chaos but Æther? The modern Ether; not such as is recognized by our scientists, but such as it was known to the ancient philosophers, long before the time of Moses; Ether, with all its mysterious and occult properties, containing in itself the germs of universal creation; Ether, the celestial virgin, the spiritual mother of every existing form and being, from whose bosom as soon as "incubated" by the Divine Spirit, are called into existence Matter and Life, Force and Action. Electricity, magnetism, heat, light, and chemical action are so little understood even now that fresh facts are constantly widening the range of our knowledge. Who knows where ends the power of this protean giant--Ether; or whence its mysterious origin?--Who, we mean, that denies the spirit that works in it and evolves out of it all visible forms?" —H.P.Blavatsky, *Isis Unveiled*

"The Astral Light is the battlefield between white and black magicians. The Astral Light is the clue of all empires and the key of all powers. It is the great universal agent of life. All the columns of angels and demons live within the Astral Light..." —Samael Aun Weor, *The Revolution of Beelzebub*

Atom: While modern science studies atoms as the basic unit of matter, they are ignoring the two other essential aspects of each atom: energy and consciousness.

"Every atom is a trio of matter, energy and consciousness. The consciousness of every atom is always an intelligent elemental. If the materialists are not capable of seeing those elementals, it is because they still do not know the scientific procedures that allow us to see them. We have special methods in order to see those creatures. Indeed, the atom is a truly infinitely small planetary system. Those planetary systems of the atoms are formed by ultra-atomic ternaries that spin around their centers of gravitation. The atom with its Alpha, Beta, and Gamma rays is a trio of matter, energy and consciousness." —Samael Aun Weor, *Sexology, the Basis of Endocrinology and Criminology*

Thus understood as being more than mere matter, atoms have great significance for all living creatures, since atoms form the basis for all living things. That is why the spiritual classic *The Dayspring of Youth* by M explains that atoms are "Minute bodies of intelligence possessing the dual attributes of Nature and man." While there are many types and levels of such atomic intelligences, both positive and negative, some of particular importance are Aspiring atoms, Destructive atoms, the Nous atom, Informer atoms, Scholar atoms, etc.

"Life will not be fully understood until we recognise the living forces within us and transplant atoms of a higher nature into the body. This will eventually help humanity to become the personification of justice. Our atomic centres are similar to the starry clusters in the sky, and each atom is a minute intelligence revolving within its own atmosphere. When we aspire we unite ourselves to atoms that have preceded us in evolution; for they evolve as we evolve: this body being their university, and they prepare the path for us to follow." —*The Dayspring of Youth* by M

"The atom of the Father is situated in the root of the nose; this is the atom of willpower. The seven serpents ascend by means of willpower, by dominating the animal impulse. The atom of the Father is situated in the root of the nose; this is the atom of willpower. The seven serpents ascend by means of willpower, by dominating the animal impulse. The atom of the Son is in the pituitary gland, whose exponent is the Nous atom (the Son of Man) in the heart. The angelic atom of the Holy Spirit shines in the pineal gland, within the chakra Sahasrara. The atom of the Father governs or controls the right ganglionary chord Pingala within which the solar atoms, the positive force, ascends. The atom of the Son governs the Sushumna canal, within which the neutral forces ascend. The atom of the Holy Spirit governs the Ida canal, within which the negative forces ascend. This is why it is related with our creative sexual forces and with the rays of the moon, which are intimately related with the reproduction of the races. Each of the seven chakras from the spinal medulla is governed by an angelic atom." —Samael Aun Weor, *Kabbalah of the Mayan Mysteries*

Auric embryo: The symbiosis of the forces of heaven and the earth crystallized within the superlative consciousness of the Being by means of their Self-realization.

"When the ego is destroyed, the Auric Embryo is formed; then the immortal principles enter into the Initiate..." —Samael Aun Weor, *Tarot and Kabbalah*

Bodhisattva: (Sanskrit) Literally, the Sanskrit term bodhi means "enlightened, wisdom, perfect knowledge," while sattva means "essence, goodness." Therefore, the term bodhisattva literally means "essence of wisdom."

A bodhisattva is a human soul (consciousness) who is on the direct path. A bodhisattva is the messenger or servant of their inner Being / Buddha.

The inner Being or Buddha resides in the superior worlds, and sends the bodhisattva into the lower worlds to work for others.

"The bodhisattva is the human soul of a master. The master is the internal God [Atman, the Innermost Buddha]." —Samael Aun Weor, *The Aquarian Message*

One becomes a bodhisattva upon:

- creating the solar bodies (astral, mental, causal) through sexual transmutation

- choosing to enter the direct path to the absolute rather than the slower spiral path

- having developed sufficient Bodhichitta (love for others in combination with comprehension of the absolute)

The word bodhisattva is a title or honorific that describes a level of consciousness earned through internal initiation, not physical. A bodhisattva is a person who through dedication to compassionate service to humanity has some degree of Bodhichitta — a psychological quality uniting deep compassion with profound insight into the nature of reality, the Absolute — and has also created the solar bodies, which correspond to the first five serpents of kundalini (candali).

In Tibetan Buddhism the term bodhisattva is sometimes publicly used in a more "generous" way to include those who aspire to become bodhisattvas.

The Tibetan translation of bodhisattva is jangchub sempa. Jangchub (Sanskrit bodhi) means "enlightenment," and sempa (Sanskrit sattva) means "hero" or a being, therefore meaning "enlightened hero." The word jangchub is from jang, "the overcoming and elimination of all obstructive forces," and chub, "realization of full knowledge." Sempa is a reference to great compassion.

"...bodhisattvas are beings who, out of intense compassion, never shift their attention away from sentient beings; they are perpetually concerned for the welfare of all beings, and they dedicate themselves entirely to securing that welfare. Thus the very name bodhisattva indicates a being who, through wisdom, heroically focuses on the attainment of enlightenment out of compassionate concern for all beings. The word itself conveys the key qualities of such an infinitely altruistic being." —The 14th Dalai Lama

"We, the bodhisattvas of compassion who love humanity immensely, state: as long as there is a single tear in any human eye, as long as there is even one suffering heart, we refuse to accept the happiness of Nirvana... We must seek the means to become more and more useful to this wretched, suffering humanity." —Samael Aun Weor, *The Major Mysteries*

Strictly speaking, the term bodhisattva addresses not a physical person but the human soul of someone walking the Direct Path. The bodhisttva is the human soul (Tipereth, the causal body), which is the servant or messenger of the inner Being (Chesed). The human soul earns the title bodhisattva by —because of love for humanity — choosing to advance spiritually by entering the terrifying Direct Path instead of the easier Spiral Path, a choice that is made only after finishing the Fifth Initiation of Fire (Tiphereth, causal body). By means of this sacrifice, this individual incarnates the Christ (Chenresig, Kuan Yin, Avalokitesvara), thereby embodying the supreme source of wisdom and compassion. That human soul is then a mixture of the divine and human, and by carrying that light within becomes a messenger or active exponent of the light. The Direct Path demands rapid and complete liberation from the ego, a route that only very few take, due to the fact that one must pay the entirety of one's karma imminently. Those who have taken this road have been the most remarkable figures in human history: Jesus, Buddha, Mohamed, Krishna, Moses, Padmasambhava, Milarepa, Joan of Arc, Fu-Xi, and many others whose names are not remembered or known.

Even among bodhisattvas there are many levels of Being: to be a bodhisattva does not mean that one is enlightened. In fact, there are many fallen bodhisattvas: human souls who resumed poor behavior and are thus cut off from their inner Being.

"Let no one seek his own good, but the good of his neighbor." —1 Corinthians 10.24

"The truly humble Bodhisattva never praises himself. The humble Bodhisattva says, 'I am just a miserable slug from the mud of the earth, I am a nobody. My person has no value. The work is what is worthy.' The Bodhisattva is the human soul of a Master. The Master is the internal God." —Samael Aun Weor, *The Aquarian Message*

"Let it be understood that a Bodhisattva is a seed, a germ, with the possibility of transcendental, divine development by means of pressure coming from the Height." —Samael Aun Weor, *The Gnostic Bible: The Pistis Sophia Unveiled*

Interestingly, the Christ in Hebrew is called Chokmah, which means "wisdom," and in Sanskrit the same is Vishnu, the root of the word "wisdom." It is Vishnu who sent his Avatars into the world in order to aid humanity. These avatars were Krishna, Buddha, Rama, and the Avatar of this age: the Avatar Kalki.

Chakra: (Sanskrit) Literally, "wheel." The chakras are subtle centers of energetic transformation. There are hundreds of chakras in our hidden physiology, but seven primary ones related to the awakening of consciousness.

"The Chakras are centres of Shakti as vital force... The Chakras are not perceptible to the gross senses. Even if they were perceptible in the living body which they help to organise, they disappear with the disintegration of organism at death." —Swami Sivananda, *Kundalini Yoga*

"The chakras are points of connection through which the divine energy circulates from one to another vehicle of the human being." —Samael Aun Weor, *Aztec Christic Magic*

Chastity: Although modern usage has rendered the term chastity virtually meaningless to most people, its original meaning and usage clearly indicate "moral purity" upon the basis of "sexual purity." Contemporary usage implies "repression" or "abstinence," which have nothing to do with real chastity. True chastity is a rejection of impure sexuality. True chastity is pure sexuality, or the activity of sex in harmony with our true nature, as explained in the secret doctrine. Properly used, the word chastity refers to sexual fidelity or honor.

"The generative energy, which, when we are loose, dissipates and makes us unclean, when we are continent invigorates and inspires us. Chastity is the flowering of man; and what are called Genius, Heroism, Holiness, and the like, are but various fruits which succeed it." —Henry David Thoreau, *Walden*

Christ: Derived from the Greek Christos, "the Anointed One," and Krestos, whose esoteric meaning is "fire." The word Christ is a title, not a personal name.

"Indeed, Christ is a Sephirothic Crown (Kether, Chokmah and Binah) of incommensurable wisdom, whose purest atoms shine within Chokmah, the world of the Ophanim. Christ is not the Monad, Christ is not the Theosophical Septenary; Christ is not the Jivan-Atman. Christ is the Central Sun. Christ is the ray that unites us to the Absolute." —Samael Aun Weor, *Tarot and Kabbalah*

"The Gnostic Church adores the saviour of the world, Jesus. The Gnostic Church knows that Jesus incarnated Christ, and that is why they adore him. Christ is not a human nor a divine individual. Christ is a title given to all fully self-realized masters. Christ is the Army of the Voice. Christ is the Verb. The Verb is far beyond the body, the soul and the Spirit. Everyone who is able to incarnate the Verb receives in fact the title of Christ. Christ is the Verb itself. It is necessary for everyone of us to incarnate the Verb (Word). When the Verb becomes flesh in us we speak with the verb of light. In actuality, several masters have incarnated the Christ. In secret India, the Christ Yogi Babaji has lived for millions of years; Babaji is immortal. The great master of wisdom Kout Humi also incarnated the Christ. Sanat Kumara, the founder of the great College of Initiates of the White Lodge, is another living Christ. In the past, many incarnated the Christ. In the present, some have incarnated the Christ. In the future many will incarnate the Christ. John the Baptist also incarnated the Christ. John the Baptist is a living Christ. The difference between Jesus and the other masters that also incarnated the Christ has to do with hierarchy. Jesus is the highest Solar initiate of the cosmos..." —Samael Aun Weor, *The Perfect Matrimony*

Consciousness: The modern English term consciousness is derived primarily from the Latin word conscius, "knowing, aware." Thus, consciousness is the basic factor of perception and understanding, and is therefore the basis of any living thing. Since living things are not equal and have a great deal of variety, so too does consciousness: it has infinite potential for development, either towards the heights of perfection or towards the depths of degeneration.

"Wherever there is life, there is consciousness. Consciousness is inherent to life as humidity is inherent to water." —Samael Aun Weor, *Sexology, the Basis of Endocrinology and Criminology*

"It is vital to understand and develop the conviction that consciousness has the potential to increase to an infinite degree." —The 14th Dalai Lama

"Light and consciousness are two phenomena of the same thing; to a lesser degree of consciousness, corresponds a lesser degree of light; to a greater degree of consciousness, a greater degree of light." —Samael Aun Weor, *The Esoteric Treatise of Hermetic Astrology*

Devolution: (Latin) From devolvere: backwards evolution, degeneration. The natural mechanical inclination for all matter and energy in nature to return towards their state of inert uniformity. Related to the Arcanum Ten: Retribution, the Wheel of Samsara. Devolution is the inverse process of evolution. As evolution is the complication of matter or energy, devolution is the slow process of nature to simplify matter or energy by applying forces to it. Through devolution, protoplasmic matter and energy descend, degrade, and increase in density within the infradimensions of nature to finally reach the center of the earth where they attain their ultimate state of inert uniformity. Devolution transfers the psyche, moral values, consciousness, or psychological responsibilities to inferior degradable organisms (Klipoth) through the surrendering of our psychological values to animal behaviors, especially sexual degeneration.

Divine Mother: The Divine Mother is the eternal, feminine principle, which is formless, and further unfolds into many levels, aspects, and manifestations.

"Devi or Sakti is the Mother of Nature. She is Nature Itself. The whole world is Her body. Mountains are Her bones. Rivers are Her veins. Ocean is Her bladder. Sun, moon are Her eyes. Wind is Her breath. Agni is Her mouth. She runs this world show. Sakti is symbolically female; but It is, in reality, neither male nor female. It is only a Force which manifests Itself in various forms. The five elements and their combinations are the external manifestations of the Mother. Intelligence, discrimination, psychic power, and will are Her internal manifestations." —Swami Sivananda

"Among the Aztecs, she was known as Tonantzin, among the Greeks as chaste Diana. In Egypt she was Isis, the Divine Mother, whose veil no mortal has lifted. There is no doubt at all that esoteric Christianity has never forsaken the worship of the Divine Mother Kundalini. Obviously she is Marah, or better said, RAM-IO, MARY. What orthodox religions did not specify, at least with regard to the exoteric or public circle, is the aspect of Isis in her individual human form. Clearly, it was taught only in secret to the Initiates that this Divine Mother exists individually within each human being. It cannot be emphasized enough that Mother-God,

Rhea, Cybele, Adonia, or whatever we wish to call her, is a variant of our own individual Being in the here and now. Stated explicitly, each of us has our own particular, individual Divine Mother." —Samael Aun Weor, *The Great Rebellion*

"Devi Kundalini, the Consecrated Queen of Shiva, our personal Divine Cosmic Individual Mother, assumes five transcendental mystic aspects in every creature, which we must enumerate:

1. The unmanifested Prakriti

2. The chaste Diana, Isis, Tonantzin, Maria or better said Ram-Io

3. The terrible Hecate, Persephone, Coatlicue, queen of the infemos and death; terror of love and law

4. The special individual Mother Nature, creator and architect of our physical organism

5. The Elemental Enchantress to whom we owe every vital impulse, every instinct." —Samael Aun Weor, *The Secret of the Golden Flower*

Ego: The multiplicity of contradictory psychological elements that we have inside are in their sum the "ego." Each one is also called "an ego" or an "I." Every ego is a psychological defect which produces suffering. The ego is three (related to our Three Brains or three centers of psychological processing), seven (capital sins), and legion (in their infinite variations).

"The ego is the root of ignorance and pain." —Samael Aun Weor, *The Esoteric Treatise of Hermetic Astrology*

"The Being and the ego are incompatible. The Being and the ego are like water and oil. They can never be mixed... The annihilation of the psychic aggregates (egos) can be made possible only by radically comprehending our errors through meditation and by the evident Self-reflection of the Being." —Samael Aun Weor, *The Pistis Sophia Unveiled*

Elementals: Creatures who have not yet created the soul; in other words, they have consciousness ("anima," raw, unformed soul) as given by nature, and have evolved mechanically through the lower kingdoms. Their physical bodies are minerals, plants, animals, and humanoids (intellectual animals); internally they have the appearance of people (gnomes, sprites, elves, fairies, mermaids, dwarves). However, in common usage the term elementals refers to the creatures of the three lower kingdoms: mineral, plant and animal, and out of politeness we call the intellectual animals "human," even though they have not become human yet.

"Just as visible Nature is populated by an infinite number of living creatures, so, according to Paracelsus, the invisible, spiritual counterpart of visible Nature (composed of the tenuous principles of the visible elements) is inhabited by a host of peculiar beings, to whom he has given the name elementals, and which have later been termed the Nature spirits. Paracelsus divided these people of the elements into four distinct groups, which he called gnomes, undines, sylphs, and salamanders. He taught that they were really living entities, many resembling human beings in shape, and inhabiting worlds of their own, unknown to man because his undeveloped senses were incapable of functioning beyond the limitations of the grosser elements. The civilizations of Greece, Rome, Egypt, China, and India believed implicitly in satyrs, sprites, and goblins. They peopled the sea with mermaids, the rivers and fountains with nymphs, the air with fairies, the fire with Lares and Penates, and the earth with fauns, dryads, and hamadryads. These Nature spirits were held in the highest esteem, and propitiatory offerings were made to them. Occasionally, as the result of atmospheric conditions or the peculiar sensitiveness of the devotee, they became visible." —Manly P. Hall, *The Secret Teachings of All Ages*

"Each elemental of Nature represents certain powers of the blessed goddess mother of the world. Thus, whosoever knows how to handle the powers of nature that are enclosed within each herb, within each root and each tree, is the only one who can be a true magician and doctor. Thought is a great force, yet everything is dual in creation. Thus, if we want to make perceptible any hidden intention, a physical instrument that serves as the clothing for that idea is necessary. This instrument is the plant that corresponds to our intention. Only the one who knows the secret of commanding the elementals of plants can be a magician." — Samael Aun Weor, *Esoteric Medicine and Practical Magic*

Elohim: [אלהים] An Hebrew term with a wide variety of meanings. In Christian translations of scripture, it is one of many words translated to the generic word "God," but whose actual meaning depends upon the context. For example:

1. In Kabbalah, אלהים is a name of God the relates to many levels of the Tree of Life. In the world of Atziluth, the word is related to divnities of the sephiroth Binah (Jehovah Elohim, mentioned especially in Genesis), Geburah, and Hod. In the world of Briah, it is related beings of Netzach and Hod.

2. El [אל] is "god," Eloah [אלה] is "goddess," therefore the plural Elohim refers to "gods and goddesses," and is commonly used to refer to Cosmo-creators or Dhyan-Choans.

3. אלה Elah or Eloah is "goddess." Yam [ים] is "sea" or "ocean." Therefore אלהים Elohim can be אלה-ים "the sea goddess" [i.e. Aphrodite, Stella Maris, etc.]

There are many more meanings of "Elohim." In general, Elohim refers to high aspects of divinity.

"Each one of us has his own Interior Elohim. The Interior Elohim is the Being of our Being. The Interior Elohim is our Father-Mother. The Interior Elohim is the ray that emanates from Aelohim." —Samael Aun Weor, *The Gnostic Bible: The Pistis Sophia Unveiled*

Essence: From Chinese 體 ti, which literally means "substance, body" and is often translated as "essence," to indicate that which is always there throughout transformations. In gnosis, the term essence refers to our consciousness, which remains fundamentally the same, in spite of the many transformations it suffers, especially life, death, and being trapped in psychological defects. A common example given in Buddhism is a glass of water: even if filled with dirt and impurities, the water is still there; its original pure essence is latent and ultimately unchanged by the presence of filth. However, one would not want to drink it that way. Just so with the Essence (the consciousness): our Essence is trapped in impurities; to use it properly, it must be cleaned first.

"Singularly radiating is the wondrous Light;
Free is it from the bondage of matter and the senses.
Not binding by words and letters.
The Essence [體] is nakedly exposed in its pure eternity.
Never defiled is the Mind-nature;
It exists in perfection from the very beginning.
By merely casting away your delusions
The Suchness of Buddhahood is realized." —Shen Tsan

"Zen, however, is interested not in these different "fields" but only in penetrating to 體 the Essence, or the innermost core of the mind for it holds that once this core is grasped, all else will become relatively insignificant, and crystal clear... only by transcending [attachment] may one come to the innermost core of Mind—the perfectly free and thoroughly nonsubstantial illuminating-Voidness. This illuminating-Void character, empty yet dynamic, is the Essence (Chinese: 體 ti) of the mind... The Essence of mind is the Illuminating-Void Suchness." —G.C.Chang, The Practice of Zen (1959)

"Without question the Essence, or consciousness, which is the same thing, sleeps deeply... The Essence in itself is very beautiful. It came from above, from the stars. Lamentably, it is smothered deep within all these "I's" we carry inside. By contrast, the Essence can retrace its steps, return to the point of origin, go back to the stars, but first it must liberate itself from its evil companions, who have trapped it within the slums of perdition. Human beings have three percent free Essence, and the other ninety-seven percent is imprisoned within the "I's"." —Samael Aun Weor, The Great Rebellion

"A percentage of psychic Essence is liberated when a defect is disintegrated. Thus, the psychic Essence which is bottled up within our defects will be completely liberated when we disintegrate each and every one of our false values, in other words, our defects. Thus, the radical transformation of ourselves will occur when the totality of our Essence is liberated. Then, in that precise moment, the eternal values of the Being will express themselves through us. Unquestionably, this would be marvelous not only for us, but also for all of humanity." —Samael Aun Weor, The Revolution of the Dialectic

Evolution: "It is not possible for the true human being (the Self-realized Being) to appear through the mechanics of evolution. We know very well that evolution and its twin sister devolution are nothing else but two laws which constitute the mechanical axis of all Nature. One evolves to a certain perfectly defined point, and then the devolving process follows. Every ascent is followed by a descent and vice-versa." —Samael Aun Weor, *Treatise of Revolutionary Psychology.*

"Evolution is a process of complication of energy." —Samael Aun Weor, *The Perfect Matrimony*

Fohat: (Theosophical/Tibetan) A term used by H.P. Blavatsky to represent the active (male) potency of the Shakti (female sexual power) in nature, the essence of cosmic electricity, vital force. As explained in *The Secret Doctrine*, "He (Fohat) is, metaphysically, the objectivised thought of the gods; the "Word made flesh" on a lower scale, and the messenger of Cosmic and human ideations: the active force in Universal Life.... In India, Fohat is connected with Vishnu and Surya in the early character of the (first) God; for Vishnu is not a high god in the Rig Veda. The name Vishnu is from the root vish, "to pervade," and Fohat is called the "Pervader" and the Manufacturer, because he shapes the atoms from crude material..." The term fohat has recently been linked with the Tibetan verb phro-wa and the noun spros-pa. These two terms are listed in Jäschke's Tibetan-English Dictionary (1881) as, for phro-wa, "to proceed, issue, emanate from, to spread, in most cases from rays of light..." while for spros-pa he gives "business, employment, activity."

Fornication: Originally, the term fornication was derived from the Indo-European word gwher, whose meanings relate to heat and burning. Fornication means to make the heat (solar fire) of the seed (sexual power) leave the body through voluntary orgasm. Any voluntary orgasm is fornication, whether between a married man and woman, or an unmarried man and woman, or through masturbation, or in any other case; this is explained by Moses: "A man from whom there is a discharge of semen, shall immerse all his flesh in water, and he shall remain unclean until evening. And any garment or any leather [object] which has semen on it, shall be immersed in water, and shall remain unclean until evening. A woman with whom a man cohabits, whereby there was [a discharge of] semen, they shall immerse in water, and they shall remain unclean until evening." —Leviticus 15:16-18

Primarily, to fornicate is to spill the sexual energy through the orgasm. Those who "deny themselves" restrain the sexual energy, and "walk in the midst of the fire" without being burned. Those who restrain the sexual energy, who renounce the orgasm, remember God in themselves, and do not defile themselves with animal passion, "for the temple of God is holy, which temple ye are."

"Whosoever is born of God doth not commit sin; for his seed remaineth in him: and he cannot sin, because he is born of God." —1 John 3:9

This is why neophytes always took a vow of sexual abstention, so that they could prepare themselves for marriage, in which they would have sexual relations but not release the sexual energy through the orgasm. This is why Paul advised:

"...they that have wives be as though they had none..." —I Corinthians 7:29

"A fornicator is an individual who has intensely accustomed his genital organs to copulate (with orgasm). Yet, if the same individual changes his custom of copulation to the custom of no copulation, then he transforms himself into a chaste person. We have as an example the astonishing case of Mary Magdalene, who was a famous prostitute. Mary Magdalene became the famous Saint Mary Magdalene, the repented prostitute. Mary Magdalene became the chaste disciple of Christ." —Samael Aun Weor, *The Revolution of Beelzebub*

Gnosis: (Greek) Knowledge.

1. The word Gnosis refers to the knowledge we acquire through our own experience, as opposed to knowledge that we are told or believe in. Gnosis - by whatever name in history or culture - is conscious, experiential knowledge, not merely intellectual or conceptual knowledge, belief, or theory. This term is synonymous with the Hebrew "daath" and the Sanskrit "jna."

2. The tradition that embodies the core wisdom or knowledge of humanity.

"Gnosis is the flame from which all religions sprouted, because in its depth Gnosis is religion. The word "religion" comes from the Latin word "religare," which implies "to link the Soul to God"; so Gnosis is the very pure flame from where all religions sprout, because Gnosis is knowledge, Gnosis is wisdom." —Samael Aun Weor from the lecture entitled *The Esoteric Path*

"The secret science of the Sufis and of the Whirling Dervishes is within Gnosis. The secret doctrine of Buddhism and of Taoism is within Gnosis. The sacred magic of the Nordics is within Gnosis. The wisdom of Hermes, Buddha, Confucius, Mohammed and Quetzalcoatl, etc., etc., is within Gnosis. Gnosis is the doctrine of Christ." —Samael Aun Weor, *The Revolution of Beelzebub*

Gunas: (Sanskrit) Literally, "fundamental quality."

"Prakriti is composed of the three Gunas or forces, namely, Sattva, Rajas and Tamas. Sattva is harmony or light or wisdom or equilibrium or goodness. Rajas is passion or motion or activity. Tamas is inertia or inaction or darkness. During Cosmic Pralaya these three Gunas exist in a state of equilibrium. During Srishti or projection a vibration arises and the three qualities are manifested in the physical universe." —Swami Sivananda, *Kundalini Yoga*

Hermaphrodite: (Greek) In the pure esoteric tradition (not the modern, degenerated remnants), hermaphrodite means "a child of Hermes and Aphrodite" (Herm-Aphrodite), one who physically develops the brain power, objective reasoning (Hermes) by means of the transmutation of its own sexual libido (Aphrodite).

Physically, hermaphrodite refers to the human being of the Lemurian epoch, who developed both male and female sexual organs and characteristics in the physical body and who was capable of reproducing its species without the necessity of sexual intercourse. A true hermaphrodite produces both sperm and ovum, and reproduces by fecundating one egg with one sperm.

Esoterically, the word hermaphrodite can refer to those who have developed spiritually to the point that they no longer require sexual cooperation.

Hydrogen: (From *hydro-* water, *gen-* generate, genes, genesis, etc.) The hydrogen is the simplest element on the periodic table and in Gnosticism it is recognized as the element that is the building block of all forms of matter. Hydrogen is a packet of solar light. The solar light (the light that comes from the sun) is the reflection of the Okidanok, the Cosmic Christ, which creates and sustains every world. This element is the fecundated water, generated water (hydro). The water is the source of all life. Everything that we eat, breathe and all of the impressions that we receive are in the form of various structures of hydrogen. Samael Aun Weor often will place a note (Do, Re, Mi...) and a number related with the vibration and atomic weight (level of complexity) with a particular hydrogen. For example, Samael Aun Weor constantly refers to the Hydrogen Si-12. "Si" is the highest note in the octave and it is the result of the notes that come before it. This particular hydrogen is always related to the forces of Yesod, which is the synthesis and coagulation of all food, air and impressions that we have previously received. Food begins at Do-768, air begins at Do-384, and impressions begin at Do-48.

Initiation: The process whereby the Innermost (the Inner Father) receives recognition, empowerment and greater responsibilities in the Internal Worlds, and little by little approaches His goal: complete Self-realization, or in other words, the return into the Absolute. Initiation NEVER applies to the "I" or our terrestrial personality.

"There are nine Initiations of Minor Mysteries and seven great Initiations of Major Mysteries. The INNERMOST is the one who receives all of these Initiations. The Testament of Wisdom says: "Before the dawning of the false aurora upon the earth, the ones who survived the hurricane and the tempest were praising the INNERMOST, and the heralds of the aurora appeared unto them." The psychological "I" does not receives Initiations. The human personality does not receive anything. Nonetheless, the "I" of some Initiates becomes filled with pride when saying 'I am a Master, I have such Initiations.' Thus, this is how the "I" believes itself to be an Initiate and keeps reincarnating in order to "perfect itself", but, the "I" never ever perfects itself. The "I" only reincarnates in order to satisfy desires. That is all." —Samael Aun Weor, *The Aquarian Message*

Initiations of Major Mysteries: The qualifications of the consciousness as it ascends into greater degrees of wisdom. The first five Initiations of Major Mysteries correspond to the creation of the real Human Being. Learn more by studying these books by Samael Aun Weor: *The Perfect Matrimony, The Three Mountains,* and *The Revolution of Beelzebub.*

"High initiation is the fusion of two principles: Atman-Buddhi, through the five principal Initiations of Major Mysteries. With the first we achieve the fusion of Atman-Buddhi, and with the fifth, we add the Manas to this fusion, and so the septenary is reduced to a trinity: "Atman-Buddhi Manas." There are a total of Nine Initiations of Major Mysteries." —Samael Aun Weor, *The Zodiacal Course*

"We fulfill our human evolution with the five Initiations of Major Mysteries. The remaining three Initiations and the degree of "Lord of the World" are of a "Super-Human" nature." —Samael Aun Weor, *Esoteric Medicine and Practical Magic*

Initiations of Minor Mysteries: The probationary steps required of all who wish to enter into the path of Self-realization. These nine tests are given to all disciples who begin to perform the Gnostic work in themselves. Only those who complete these tests can receive the right to enter into the Major Mysteries. For more information, read *The Perfect Matrimony.*

"Remember that each one of the nine Initiations of Lesser Mysteries has a musical note and an instrument which produces it." —Samael Aun Weor, *The Revolution of Beelzebub*

"To want to rapidly become fused with the Innermost without having passed through the nine initiations of Lesser Mysteries is akin to wanting to receive a doctor's degree in medicine without having studied all the required years at university, or like wanting to be a general without having passed through all the military ranks." —Samael Aun Weor, *The Zodiacal Course*

"Throughout the Initiations of Lesser Mysteries, the disciple has to pass through the entire tragedy of Golgotha..." —Samael Aun Weor, *The Zodiacal Course*

Innermost: "Our real Being is of a universal nature. Our real Being is neither a kind of superior nor inferior "I." Our real Being is impersonal, universal, divine. He transcends every concept of "I," me, myself, ego, etc., etc." —Samael Aun Weor, *The Perfect Matrimony*

Also known as Atman, the Spirit, Chesed, our own individual interior divine Father.

"The Innermost is the ardent flame of Horeb. In accordance with Moses, the Innermost is the Ruach Elohim (the Spirit of God) who sowed the waters in the beginning of the world. He is the Sun King, our Divine Monad, the Alter-Ego of Cicerone." —Samael Aun Weor, *The Revolution of Beelzebub*

Intellectual Animal: The current state of humanity: animals with intellect.

When the Intelligent Principle, the Monad, sends its spark of consciousness into Nature, that spark, the anima, enters into manifestation as a simple mineral. Gradually, over millions of years, the anima gathers experience and evolves up the chain of life until it perfects itself in the level of the mineral kingdom. It then graduates into the plant kingdom, and subsequently into the animal kingdom. With each ascension the spark receives new capacities and higher grades of complexity. In the animal kingdom it learns procreation by ejaculation. When that animal intelligence enters into the human kingdom, it receives a new capacity: reasoning, the intellect; it is now an anima with intellect: an Intellectual Animal. That spark must then perfect itself in the human kingdom in order to become a complete and perfect human being, an entity that has conquered and transcended everything that belongs to the lower kingdoms. Unfortunately, very few intellectual animals perfect themselves; most remain enslaved by their animal nature, and thus are reabsorbed by Nature, a process belonging to the devolving side of life and called by all the great religions "Hell" or the Second Death.

"The present manlike being is not yet human; he is merely an intellectual animal. It is a very grave error to call the legion of the "I" the "soul." In fact, what the manlike being has is the psychic material, the material for the soul within his Essence, but indeed, he does not have a Soul yet." — Samael Aun Weor, *The Revolution of the Dialectic*

Internal Worlds: The many dimensions beyond the physical world. These dimensions are both subjective and objective. To know the objective internal worlds (the astral plane, or Nirvana, or the Klipoth) one must first know one's own personal, subjective internal worlds, because the two are intimately associated.

"Whosoever truly wants to know the internal worlds of the planet Earth or of the solar system or of the galaxy in which we live, must previously know his intimate world, his individual, internal life, his own internal worlds. Man, know thyself, and thou wilt know the universe and its gods. The more we explore this internal world called "myself," the more we will comprehend that we simultaneously live in two worlds, in two realities, in two confines: the external and the internal. In the same way that it is indispensable for one to learn how to walk in the external world so as not to fall down into a precipice, or not get lost in the streets of the city, or to select one's friends, or not associate with the perverse ones, or not eat poison, etc.; likewise, through the psychological work upon oneself we learn how to walk in the internal world, which is explorable only through Self-observation." —Samael Aun Weor, *Treatise of Revolutionary Psychology*

Through the work in Self-observation, we develop the capacity to awaken where previously we were asleep: including in the objective internal worlds.

Kali: Sanskrit "the black one, night, goddess of time, strife." In the sacred Vedas, this name refers to one of the seven tongues of Agni, the god of fire. The meaning has since changed to refer to the goddess Kali, the consort of Shiva. The name Kali is derived from ka, the first consonant of Sanskrit, and which can mean "time, pleasure, light, sound, sun, air, soul, wealth, water, head, fire, body," and much more. Further, kā means "seek, desire, yearn, love." The second syllable lī means "to melt, liquefy, dissolve." Thus, in Tantra, the goddess Kali represents the power that can dissolve desire. Desire is the glue that binds us to suffering. Conversely, in negative forms of Tantra, Kali is worshipped as a fulfiller of desire, that which binds us to lust.

"In India, Kali the Divine Mother Kundalini is adored, but Kali in her black, fatal aspect is also adored. These are the two Marys, the white and the black. The two Serpents, the Serpent of Brass which healed the Israelites in the wilderness and the Tempting Serpent of Eden." —Samael Aun Weor, *The Perfect Matrimony*

Karma: (Sanskrit, literally "deed"; derived from kri, "to do...") The law of cause and effect.

"Be not deceived; God is not mocked: for whatsoever a man soweth, that shall he also reap." —Galatians 6:7

Kundabuffer: Originally a useful organ that served the function of helping ancient humanity become focused on material, physical existence, it became corrupted by desire and sexual fall, thus resulting in the emergence of the ego and the fortification of the sexual energy in a negative polarity, and has since been symbolized by the tail of the devils, the tail of Satan.

"It is necessary to know that the Kundabuffer organ is the negative development of the fire. This is the descending serpent, which precipitates itself from the coccyx downwards, towards the atomic infernos of the human being. The Kundabuffer organ is the horrifying tail of Satan, which is shown in the "body of desires" of the intellectual animal, who in the present times is falsely called human." —Samael Aun Weor, *The Elimination of Satan's Tail*

"The diabolic type whose seduction is here, there and everywhere under the pretext of working in the Ninth Sphere, who abandons his wife because he thinks she will not be useful to him for the work in the fiery forge of Vulcan, instead of awakening Kundalini, will awaken the abominable Kundabuffer organ. A certain Initiate, whose name will not be mentioned in this treatise, commits the error of attributing to the Kundalini all the sinister qualities of the Kundabuffer organ... When the Fire is cast downwards from the chakra of the coccyx, the tail of Satan appears; the abominable Kundabuffer organ. The hypnotic power of the organ of Witches' Sabbath holds the human multitude asleep and depraved. Those who commit the crime of practicing Black Tantra (Sexual Magic with seminal ejaculation) clearly awaken and develop the organ of all fatalities. Those who betray their guru or master, even if practicing White Tantra (without seminal ejaculation), will obviously activate the organ of all evils. Such sinister power opens the seven doorways of the lower abdomen (the seven infernal chakras) and converts us into terribly perverse demons." —Samael Aun Weor, *The Secret of the Golden Flower*

Kundalini: "Kundalini, the serpent power or mystic fire, is the primordial energy or Sakti that lies dormant or sleeping in the Muladhara Chakra, the centre of the body. It is called the serpentine or annular power on account of serpentine form. It is an electric fiery occult power, the great pristine force which underlies all organic and inorganic matter. Kundalini is the cosmic power in individual bodies. It is not a material force like electricity, magnetism, centripetal or centrifugal force. It is a spiritual potential Sakti or cosmic power. In reality it has no form. [...] O Divine Mother Kundalini, the Divine Cosmic Energy that is hidden in men! Thou art Kali, Durga, Adisakti, Rajarajeswari, Tripurasundari, Maha-Lakshmi, Maha-Sarasvati! Thou hast put on all these names and forms. Thou hast manifested as Prana, electricity, force, magnetism, cohesion, gravitation in this universe. This whole universe rests in Thy bosom. Crores of salutations unto thee. O Mother of this world! Lead me on to open the Sushumna Nadi and take Thee along the Chakras to Sahasrara Chakra and to merge myself in Thee and Thy consort, Lord Siva. Kundalini Yoga is that Yoga which treats of Kundalini Sakti, the six centres of spiritual energy (Shat Chakras), the arousing of the sleeping Kundalini Sakti and its union with Lord Siva in Sahasrara Chakra, at the crown of the head. This is an exact science. This is also known as Laya Yoga. The six centres are pierced (Chakra Bheda) by the passing of Kundalini Sakti to the top of the head. 'Kundala' means 'coiled'. Her form is like a coiled serpent. Hence the name Kundalini." —Swami Sivananda, *Kundalini Yoga*

"Kundalini is a compound word: Kunda reminds us of the abominable "Kundabuffer organ," and lini is an Atlantean term meaning termination. Kundalini means "the termination of the abominable Kundabuffer organ." In this case, it is imperative not to confuse Kundalini with Kundabuffer." —Samael Aun Weor, *The Great Rebellion*

These two forces, one positive and ascending, and one negative and descending, are symbolized in the Bible in the book of Numbers (the story of the serpent of brass). The Kundalini is "The power of life."- from the Theosophical Glossary. The sexual fire that is at the base of all life.

"The ascent of the Kundalini along the spinal cord is achieved very slowly in accordance with the merits of the heart. The fires of the heart control the miraculous development of the sacred serpent. Devi Kundalini is not something mechanical as many suppose; the igneous serpent is only awakened with genuine Love between husband and wife, and it will never rise up along the medullar canal of adulterers." —Samael Aun Weor, *The Secret of the Golden Flower*

"The decisive factor in the progress, development and evolution of the Kundalini is ethics." —Samael Aun Weor, *The Revolution of Beelzebub*

"Until not too long ago, the majority of spiritualists believed that on awakening the Kundalini, the latter instantaneously rose to the head and the initiate was automatically united with his Innermost or Internal God, instantly, and converted into Mahatma. How comfortable! How comfortably all these theosophists, Rosicrucians and spiritualists, etc., imagined High Initiation." —Samael Aun Weor, *The Zodiacal Course*

"There are seven bodies of the Being. Each body has its "cerebrospinal" nervous system, its medulla and Kundalini. Each body is a complete organism. There are, therefore, seven bodies, seven medullae and seven Kundalinis. The ascension of each of the seven Kundalinis is slow and difficult. Each canyon or vertebra represents determined occult powers and this is why the conquest of each canyon undergoes terrible tests." — Samael Aun Weor, *The Zodiacal Course*

Laya Center: Sanskrit meaning, "point of dissolution" Laya is from the Sanskrit root li, meaning "to dissolve," "to disintegrate," or "to vanish away." A laya-center is the cosmic point where matter disappears from one dimension and passes to exist into another dimension. A laya center is the core-space through which the Logos applies the karmic law as a cause for any life in any dimension, from higher laya centers of higher parallel universes into the lower laya centers of lower manifested universes. A laya-center could be conceived as a cosmic vortex through which the Logos from superior spheres of consciousness pours down its creative energy into the lowers spheres, thus, animating, inspiring and breathing its own essence or substance into the lower parallel universes. The Logos is the cognizant or mechanical directive force or driving power of many degrees behind any laya center in any universe. Behind the laya-center of any evolving and devolving mechanism of nature stands the intelligence of the Logos. A laya-center is that core of the space where the substance becomes again homogeneous. Any given laya-center exists in between parallel universes. Any Logoic jierarchy acts through innumerable number of laya-centers.

Left-hand: In traditional cultures (especially Asian), the right hand is utilized for positive, clean, upright actions, such as eating, making offerings, etc., while the left hand is used for hidden, unclean, or harmful actions. This tradition emerged from the ancient esoteric knowledge, unknown to the public, in which the followers of the light (divinity, purity) correspond to the "right-hand of God" while the adherents of impurity and desire fall to the left, into disgrace. These contrary paths are rooted in Sanskrit terms. Dakshinachara (Sanskrit) literally means "upright in conduct" but is interpreted as "Right-Hand Path." Vamacara literally means "black magic," or "behaving badly or in the wrong way," and is used to refer to "Left-Hand Path" or "Left-path" (Sanskrit: Vamamarga). These two paths are explained in Kabbalah as well.

In modern times, those who follow the left-hand path have worked hard to make their path seem respectable and equal to the right, by claiming the two need each other to exist. This argument is based on the lie that left-hand initiates pursue the darkness of the Uncreated Light, the Absolute (which is pure, divine), yet the reality is that their degeneration and harmful acts propel them into the darkness of the abyss, the hell realms, to be cleansed of their impurity. Followers of the left-hand path believe they can outwit Divinity.

"And he shall separate them one from another, as a shepherd divideth his sheep from the goats. And he shall set the sheep on his right, but the goats on his left." —Matthew 25: 32-33

"Then the people of the right hand —Oh! how happy shall be the people of the right hand! And the people of the left hand —Oh! how wretched shall be the people of the left hand!" —Qur'an, Surah Al-Waqiah (The Inevitable) [56:8-9]

The widespread of the use of these terms in the West originated with H. P. Blavatsky.

It is important to note that physical handedness has nothing to do with one's spiritual level, value, or destiny. The persecution of left-handedness is just an ignorant form of discrimination.

"In symbolism the body is divided vertically into halves, the right half being considered as light and the left half as darkness. By those unacquainted with the true meanings of light and darkness the light half was denominated spiritual and the left half material. Light is the symbol of objectivity; darkness of subjectivity. Light is a manifestation of life and is therefore posterior to life. That which is anterior to light is darkness, in which light exists temporarily but darkness permanently. As life precedes light, its only symbol is darkness, and darkness is considered as the veil which must eternally conceal the true nature of abstract and undifferentiated Being.

"In ancient times men fought with their right arms and defended the vital centers with their left arms, on which was carried the protecting shield. The right half of the body was regarded therefore as offensive and the left half defensive. For this reason also the right side of the body was considered masculine and the left side feminine. Several authorities are of the opinion that the present prevalent right-handedness of the race is the outgrowth of the custom of holding the left hand in restraint for defensive purposes. Furthermore, as the source of Being is in the primal darkness which preceded light, so the spiritual nature of man is in the dark part of his being, for the heart is on the left side.

"Among the curious misconceptions arising from the false practice of associating darkness with evil is one by which several early nations used the right hand for all constructive labors and the left hand for only those purposes termed unclean and unfit for the sight of the gods. For the same reason black magic was often referred to as the left-hand path, and heaven was said to be upon the right and hell upon the left. Some philosophers further declared that there were two methods of writing: one from left to right, which was considered the exoteric method; the other from right to left, which was considered esoteric. The exoteric writing was that which was done out or away from the heart, while the esoteric writing was that which--like the ancient Hebrew--was written toward the heart." —Manly P. Hall, *The Secret Teachings of All Ages*

Lemuria: The people of Lemuria were the third root race of this terrestrial round. They inhabited the huge continent Mu in the Pacific Ocean. In the early stages of their time, they were hermaphrodites, yet gradually passed through the division of sexes, thus being the source of the stories in many myths and scriptures.

The Lemurians existed before the Atlanteans, but have been confused with them by some groups. About this, H.P. Blavatsky said, "In our own day we witness the stupendous fact that such comparatively recent personages as Shakespeare and William Tell are all but denied, an attempt being made to show one to be a nom de plume, and the other a person who never existed. What wonder then, that the two powerful races -- the Lemurians and the Atlanteans -- have been merged into and identified, in time, with a few half mythical peoples, who all bore the same patronymic?" (The Secret Doctrine, 1888)

"It is clear that the Miocene Epoch had its proper scenario on the ancient Lemurian land, the continent that was formerly located in the Pacific Ocean. Remnants of Lemuria are still located in Oceania, in the great Australia, and on Easter Island (where some carved monoliths were found), etc." —Samael Aun Weor, *Gnostic Anthropology*

"The third root race was the Lemurian race, which inhabited Mu, which today is the Pacific Ocean. They perished by fire raining from the sun (volcanoes and earthquakes). This Root Race was governed by the Aztec God Tlaloc. Their reproduction was by means of gemmation. Lemuria was a very extensive continent. The Lemurians who degenerated had, afterwards, faces similar to birds; this is why some savages, when remembering tradition, adorned their heads with feathers." —Samael Aun Weor, *The Kabbalah of the Mayan Mysteries*

Logos: (Greek, plural Logoi) means Verb or Word. In Greek and Hebrew metaphysics, the unifying principle of the world. The Logos is the manifested deity of every nation and people; the outward expression or the effect of the cause which is ever concealed. (Speech is the "logos" of thought). The Logos has three aspects, known universally as the Trinity or Trimurti. The First Logos is the Father, Brahma. The Second Logos is the Son, Vishnu. The Third Logos is the Holy Spirit, Shiva. One who incarnates the Logos becomes a Logos.

"The Logos is not an individual. The Logos is an army of ineffable beings." —Samael Aun Weor, *Sexology, the Basis of Endocrinology and Criminology*

Master: Like many terms related to spirituality, this one is grossly misunderstood. Although many people claim to be "masters," the truth is that the terrestrial person is only a terrestrial person. The only one who can be a master is the Innermost, Atman, the Father, Chesed.

"And, behold, one came and said unto [Jesus], Good master, what good thing shall I do, that I may have eternal life? And he said unto him, Why callest thou me good? there is none good but one, that is, God." —Matthew 19

"The value of the human person which is the intellectual animal called human being is less than the ash of a cigarette. However, the fools feel themselves to be giants. Unfortunately, within all the pseudo-esoteric currents a great amount of mythomaniac people exist, individuals who feel themselves to be masters, people who enjoy when others call them masters, individuals who believe themselves to be Gods, individuals who presume to be saints. The only one who is truly great is the Spirit, the Innermost. We, the intellectual animals, are leaves that the wind tosses about... No student of occultism is a master. True masters are only those who have reached the Fifth Initiation of Major Mysteries [Tiphereth, the causal body]. Before the Fifth Initiation nobody is a master." —Samael Aun Weor, *The Perfect Matrimony*

"You [if you have reached levels of initiation] are not the master, you are only the sinning shadow of He who has never sinned. Remember that only your internal Lamb is the master. Remember that even though your internal God is a Hierarch of fire, you, poor slug, are only a human being and as a human being you will always be judged. Your internal Lamb could be a planetary God, but you, poor slug of the mud, do not forget, always remember that you are only the shadow of your God. Poor sinning shadow..! Do not say "I am this God" or "I am that master," because you are only a shadow that must resolve to die and be slaughtered in order not to serve as an obstacle for your internal God. It is necessary for you to reach supreme humbleness." —Samael Aun Weor, *The Aquarian Message*

"Do not accept external masters in the physical plane. Learn how to travel in the astral body, and when you are skillful in the astral, choose an authentic master of Major Mysteries of the White Brotherhood and consecrate unto him the most absolute devotion and the most profound respect." —Samael Aun Weor, *The Zodiacal Course*

Meditation: "When the esotericist submerges himself into meditation, what he seeks is information." —Samael Aun Weor

"It is urgent to know how to meditate in order to comprehend any psychic aggregate, or in other words, any psychological defect. It is indispensable to know how to work with all our heart and with all our soul, if we want the elimination to occur." —Samael Aun Weor, *The Gnostic Bible: The Pistis Sophia Unveiled*

"1. The Gnostic must first attain the ability to stop the course of his thoughts, the capacity to not think. Indeed, only the one who achieves that capacity will hear the Voice of the Silence.

"2. When the Gnostic disciple attains the capacity to not think, then he must learn to concentrate his thoughts on only one thing.

"3. The third step is correct meditation. This brings the first flashes of the new consciousness into the mind.

"4. The fourth step is contemplation, ecstasy or Samadhi. This is the state of Turiya (perfect clairvoyance)." —Samael Aun Weor, *The Perfect Matrimony*

Monad: (Latin) From monas, "unity; a unit, monad." The Monad is the Being, the Innermost, our own inner Spirit.

"We must distinguish between Monads and Souls. A Monad, in other words, a Spirit, is; a Soul is acquired. Distinguish between the Monad of a world and the Soul of a world; between the Monad of a human and the Soul of a human; between the Monad of an ant and the Soul of an ant. The human organism, in final synthesis, is constituted by billions and trillions of infinitesimal Monads. There are several types and orders of primary elements of all existence, of every organism, in the manner of germs of all the phenomena of nature; we can call the latter Monads, employing the term of Leibnitz, in the absence of a more descriptive term to indicate the simplicity of the simplest existence. An atom, as a vehicle of action, corresponds to each of these genii or Monads. The Monads attract each other, combine, transform themselves, giving form to every organism, world, micro-organism, etc. Hierarchies exist among the Monads; the Inferior Monads must obey the Superior ones that is the Law. Inferior Monads belong to the Superior ones. All the trillions of Monads that animate the human organism have to obey the owner, the chief, the Principal Monad. The regulating Monad, the Primordial Monad permits the activity of all of its subordinates inside the human organism, until the time indicated by the Law of Karma." —Samael Aun Weor, *The Esoteric Treatise of Hermetic Astrology*

"(The number) one is the Monad, the Unity, Iod-Heve or Jehovah, the Father who is in secret. It is the Divine Triad that is not incarnated within a Master who has not killed the ego. He is Osiris, the same God, the Word." —Samael Aun Weor, *Tarot and Kabbalah*

"When spoken of, the Monad is referred to as Osiris. He is the one who has to Self-realize Himself... Our own particular Monad needs us and we need it. Once, while speaking with my Monad, my Monad told me, 'I am self-realizing Thee; what I am doing, I am doing for Thee.' Otherwise, why are we living? The Monad wants to Self-realize and that is why we are here. This is our objective." —Samael Aun Weor, *Tarot and Kabbalah*

"The Monads or vital genii are not exclusive to the physical organism; within the atoms of the internal bodies there are found imprisoned many orders and categories of living Monads. The existence of any physical or supersensible, angelic or diabolical, solar or lunar body, has billions and trillions of Monads as their foundation." —Samael Aun Weor, *The Esoteric Treatise of Hermetic Astrology*

Mountain of Initiation: The first of three symbolic mountains that represent stages of spiritual development. The first mountain is a series of initiations achieved by the Monad, in which the soul is created and prepared for the remainder of the work. See *The Three Mountains* by Samael Aun Weor.

Nirvana: (Sanskrit, "extinction" or "cessation"; Tibetan: nyangde, literally "the state beyond sorrow") In general use, refers to the permanent cessation of suffering and its causes, and therefore refers to a state of consciousness rather than a place. Yet, the term can also apply to heavenly realms, whose vibration is directed related to the cessation of suffering. In other words, if your mind-stream has liberated itself from the causes of suffering, it will naturally vibrate at the level of Nirvana (heaven).

"When the Soul fuses with the Inner Master, then it becomes free from Nature and enters into the supreme happiness of absolute existence. This state of happiness is called Nirvana. Nirvana can be attained through millions of births and deaths, but it can also be attained by means of a shorter path; this is the path of "initiation." The Initiate can reach Nirvana in one single life if he so wants it." —Samael Aun Weor, *The Zodiacal Course*

Root Races: "Every planet develops seven root races and seven subraces. Our planet Earth already developed five root races; it needs to develop two more root races. After the seven root races, the planet Earth, already transformed by cataclysms over the course of millions of years, will become a new moon." —Samael Aun Weor, *The Kabbalah of the Mayan Mysteries*

The seven root races of this planet Earth are:

1. Polar protoplasmatic
2. Hyperborean
3. Lemurian
4. Atlantean
5. Aryan (present)
6. Koradi (future)
7. (Seventh) (future)

Furthermore, each root race has seven subraces.

Second Death: A mechanical process in nature experienced by those souls who within the allotted time fail to reach union with their inner divinity (i.e. known as self-realization, liberation, religare, yoga, moksha, etc). The Second Death is the complete dissolution of the ego (karma, defects, sins) in the infernal regions of nature, which after unimaginable quantities of suffering, proportional to the density of the psyche, in the end purifies the Essence (consciousness) so that it may try again to perfect itself and reach the union with the Being.

"He that overcometh (the sexual passion) shall inherit all things; and I will be his God (I will incarnate myself within him), and he shall be my son (because he is a Christified one), But the fearful (the tenebrous, cowards, unbelievers), and unbelieving, and the abominable, and murderers, and whoremongers, and sorcerers, and idolaters, and all liars, shall have their part in the lake which burneth with fire and brimstone: which is the second death. (Revelation 21) This lake which burns with fire and brimstone is the lake of carnal passion. This lake is related with the lower animal depths of the human being and its atomic region is the abyss. The tenebrous slowly disintegrate themselves within the abyss until they die. This is the second death." —Samael Aun Weor, *The Aquarian Message*

"When the bridge called "Antakarana," which communicates the divine triad with its "inferior essence", is broken, the inferior essence (trapped into the ego) is left separated and is sunk into the abyss of destructive forces, where it (its ego) disintegrates little by little. This is the Second Death of which the Apocalypse speaks; this is the state of consciousness called "Avitchi." —Samael Aun Weor, *The Zodiacal Course*

"The Second Death is really painful. The ego feels as if it has been divided in different parts, the fingers fall off, its arms, its legs. It suffers through a tremendous breakdown." —Samael Aun Weor, from the lecture *The Mysteries of Life and Death*

Self-realization: The achievement of perfect knowledge. This phrase is better stated as, "The realization of the Innermost Self," or "The realization of the true nature of self." At the ultimate level, this is the experiential, conscious knowledge of the Absolute, which is synonymous with Emptiness, Shunyata, or Non-being.

Sexual Magic: The word magic is derived from the ancient word magos "one of the members of the learned and priestly class," from O.Pers. magush, possibly from PIE *magh- "to be able, to have power." [Quoted from Online Etymology Dictionary].

"All of us possess some electrical and magnetic forces within, and, just like a magnet, we exert a force of attraction and repulsion... Between lovers that magnetic force is particularly powerful and its action has a far-reaching effect." —Samael Aun Weor, *The Secret of the Golden Flower*

Sexual magic refers to an ancient science that has been known and protected by the purest, most spiritually advanced human beings, whose purpose and goal is the harnessing and perfection of our sexual forces. A more accurate translation of sexual magic would be "sexual priesthood." In ancient times, the priest was always accompanied by a priestess, for they represent the divine forces at the base of all creation: the masculine and feminine, the Yab-Yum, Ying-Yang, Father-Mother: the Elohim. Unfortunately, the term "sexual magic" has been grossly misinterpreted by mistaken persons such as Aleister Crowley, who advocated a host of degenerated practices, all of which belong solely to the lowest and most perverse mentality and lead only to the enslavement of the consciousness, the worship of lust and desire, and the decay of humanity. True, upright, heavenly sexual magic is the natural harnessing of our latent forces, making them active and harmonious with nature and the divine, and which leads to the perfection of the human being.

"People are filled with horror when they hear about sexual magic; however, they are not filled with horror when they give themselves to all kinds of sexual perversion and to all kinds of carnal passion." —Samael Aun Weor, *The Perfect Matrimony*

Solar Bodies: The physical, vital, astral, mental, and causal bodies that are created through the beginning stages of alchemy/tantra and that provide a basis for existence in their corresponding levels of nature, just as the physical body does in the physical world. These bodies or vehicles are superior due to being created out of solar (Christic) energy, as opposed to the inferior, lunar bodies we receive from nature. Also known as the Wedding Garment (Christianity), the Merkabah (Kabbalah), To Soma Heliakon (Greek), and Sahu (Egyptian).

"All the masters of the White Lodge, the angels, archangels, thrones, seraphim, virtues, etc. are garbed with the solar bodies. Only those who have solar bodies have the Being incarnated. Only someone who possesses the Being is an authentic human being." —Samael Aun Weor, *The Esoteric Treatise of Hermetic Astrology*

Tantra: Sanskrit for "continuum" or "unbroken stream." This refers first (1) to the continuum of vital energy that sustains all existence, and second (2) to the class of knowledge and practices that harnesses that vital energy, thereby transforming the practitioner. There are many schools of Tantra, but they can be classified in three types: White, Grey and Black. Tantra has long been known in the West as Alchemy.

"In the view of Tantra, the body's vital energies are the vehicles of the mind. When the vital energies are pure and subtle, one's state of mind will be accordingly affected. By transforming these bodily energies we transform the state of consciousness." —The 14th Dalai Lama

Tree of Knowledge of Good and Evil: (Hebrew) From Hebrew: עץ tree. דעת (Daath) "knowledge." טוב "goodness." רע "pollution" or "impurity." -

One of two trees in the Garden of Eden, the Tree of Knowledge in Hebrew is Daath, which is related to the sexual organs and the study of sexuality, known also as Alchemy / Tantra. The full name "Tree of Knowledge of Goodness and Impurity" indicates that Daath, sexual "knowledge," leads to either "goodness" or "impurity."

Tree of Life: (Hebrew) Although the Hebrew term is plural ("Tree of Lives") it is usually rendered singular.

"And out of the ground made the LORD God to grow every tree that is pleasant to the sight, and good for food; the tree of life also in the midst of the garden, and the tree of knowledge of good and evil." —Genesis 2:9

This tree represents the structure of the soul (microcosm) and of the universe (macrocosm).

"The Tree of Life is the spinal medulla. This tree of wisdom is also the ten sephiroth, the twenty-two creative Major Arcana, letters, sounds and numbers, with which the Logos (God) created the universe." —from Alcione, a lecture by Samael Aun Weor

White Lodge or Brotherhood: That ancient collection of pure souls who maintain the highest and most sacred of sciences: White Magic or White Tantra. It is called White due to its purity and cleanliness. This "Brotherhood" or "Lodge" includes human beings of the highest order from every race, culture, creed and religion, and of both sexes.

Yoga: (Sanskrit) "union." Similar to the Latin "religare," the root of the word "religion." In Tibetan, it is "rnal-'byor" which means "union with the fundamental nature of reality."

"The word YOGA comes from the root Yuj which means to join, and in its spiritual sense, it is that process by which the human spirit is brought into near and conscious communion with, or is merged in, the Divine Spirit, according as the nature of the human spirit is held to be separate from (Dvaita, Visishtadvaita) or one with (Advaita) the Divine Spirit." — Swami Sivananda, *Kundalini Yoga*

"Patanjali defines Yoga as the suspension of all the functions of the mind. As such, any book on Yoga, which does not deal with these three aspects of the subject, viz., mind, its functions and the method of suspending them, can be safely laid aside as unreliable and incomplete." —Swami Sivananda, *Practical Lessons In Yoga*

"The word yoga means in general to join one's mind with an actual fact..." —The 14th Dalai Lama

"The soul aspires for the union with his Innermost, and the Innermost aspires for the union with his Glorian." —Samael Aun Weor, *The Revolution of Beelzebub*

"All of the seven schools of Yoga are within Gnosis, yet they are in a synthesized and absolutely practical way. There is Tantric Hatha Yoga in the practices of the Maithuna (Sexual Magic). There is practical Raja Yoga in the work with the chakras. There is Gnana / Jnana Yoga in our practices and mental disciplines which we have cultivated in secrecy for millions of years. We have Bhakti Yoga in our prayers and Rituals. We have Laya Yoga in our meditation and respiratory exercises. Samadhi exists in our practices with the Maithuna and during our deep meditations. We live the path of Karma Yoga in our upright actions, in our upright thoughts, in our upright feelings, etc." —Samael Aun Weor, *The Revolution of Beelzebub*

"Yoga does not consist in sitting cross-legged for six hours or stopping the beatings of the heart or getting oneself buried underneath the ground for a week or a month. These are all physical feats only. Yoga is the science that teaches you the method of uniting the individual will with the Cosmic Will. Yoga transmutes the unregenerate nature and increases energy, vitality, vigour, and bestows longevity and a high standard of health." —Swami Sivananda, *Autobiography*

"Brahmacharya [sexual purity] is the very foundation of Yoga." —Swami Sivananda

"The Yoga that we require today is actually ancient Gnostic Christian Yoga, which absolutely rejects the idea of Hatha Yoga. We do not recommend Hatha Yoga simply because, spiritually speaking, the acrobatics of this discipline are fruitless; they should be left to the acrobats of the circus." —Samael Aun Weor, *The Yellow Book*

"Yoga has been taught very badly in the Western world. Multitudes of pseudo-sapient Yogis have spread the false belief that the true Yogi must be an infrasexual (an enemy of sex). Some of these false yogis have never even visited India; they are infrasexual pseudo-yogis. These ignoramuses believe that they are going to achieve in-depth realization only with the yogic exercises, such as asanas, pranayamas, etc. Not only do they have such false beliefs, but what is worse is that they propagate them; thus, they misguide many people away from the difficult, straight, and narrow door that leads unto the light. No authentically initiated Yogi from India would ever think that he could achieve his inner self-realization with pranayamas or asanas, etc. Any legitimate Yogi from India knows very well that such yogic exercises are only co-assistants that are very useful for their health and for the development of their powers, etc. Only the Westerners and pseudo-yogis have within their minds the belief that they can achieve Self-realization with such exercises. Sexual Magic is practiced very secretly within the Ashrams of India. Any true yogi initiate from India works with the Arcanum A.Z.F. This is taught by the great Yogis from India that have visited the Western world, and if it has not been taught by these great, initiated Hindustani Yogis, if it has not been published in their books of Yoga, it was in order to avoid scandals. You can be absolutely sure that the Yogis who do not practice Sexual Magic will never achieve birth in the superior worlds. Thus, whosoever affirms the contrary is a liar, an impostor." —Samael Aun Weor, *Alchemy and Kabbalah in the Tarot*

Index

Apollonius, 171
Apopi, 21
Apostles, 40, 126
Appetites, 141
Aquarian, 27, 79, 82, 104, 117, 121,
    132, 175-176, 181-182, 190,
    198, 201
Arcanum, 28, 34-35, 176, 184, 204
Archangels, 79, 202
Archetypes, 71
Arhats, 133
Arimathea, 33
Ark, 33, 176
Army, 103, 109-110, 112, 114, 183,
    197
Aroch, 90, 93
Art, 6, 14, 126, 149, 157, 194
Aryan, 81-82, 176-177, 200
Asanas, 117, 204
Ascend, 129-130, 180
Ascending, 37, 109, 116-117, 194
Ascends, 19, 41, 55, 71, 92, 115, 120,
    123, 125, 162, 180, 191
Ascension, 37, 41, 111-112, 192, 195
Ascent, 42, 145, 188, 194
Ascetic, 23
Asleep, 10, 23-25, 47, 68-69, 154,
    192-193
Aspire, 15, 180-181
Astaroth, 19
Astral, 9-10, 12-13, 24-25, 38, 82, 89,
    99, 102, 129, 133, 140-141,
    144-146, 153-155, 161, 165,
    169-172, 177-179, 181, 192,
    198, 202
Astral Body, 9-10, 12-13, 24-25, 99,
    102, 129, 140-141, 153-154,
    165, 170-171, 177, 198
Astral Light, 82, 161, 177-179
Astral Projection, 24
Astronomer, 27
Athena, 54
Atlantis, 31, 81, 135
Atman, 99, 181, 191, 197
Atmic, 146
Atmosphere, 24, 81, 120, 178, 180

Atom, 59, 95, 129, 158-159, 179-180,
    199
Atomic, 19, 59, 82, 129, 157-159,
    161-163, 166-167, 180, 190,
    193, 201
Atoms, 63, 92, 95, 107, 109, 111-112,
    120, 129-130, 157-158, 161,
    179-180, 183, 188, 199
Atrophied, 64
Attention, 63, 181
Attract, 107, 199
Aum, 162
Avalokiteshvara, 103, 109
Avatar, 104, 182
Avitchi, 142, 201
Awake, 9, 69, 116
Awaken, 7-8, 41-42, 79, 92-93, 112,
    119-120, 126, 129-130, 133,
    137, 155, 161-162, 168, 170,
    192-193
Awakened, 8, 41, 47, 50, 55, 90, 102,
    112, 179, 194
Awakening, 6, 8, 10, 23-24, 39, 41-
    43, 90, 117, 120, 124, 131,
    133, 135, 154, 182, 193-194
Awakens, 8, 10, 15, 37, 41, 87-88, 90,
    92, 120, 123, 127, 133, 135,
    137, 139, 166
Aware, 50, 183
Aztec, 35, 168, 182, 197
Babel, 50, 58
Bacchus, 30
Bamidbar, 71
Bana Linga, 143
Bandhas, 132
Baptism, 161
Baptist, 103, 183
Barbaric, 8
Beast, 11
Bed, 24, 68, 145, 147, 154, 170
Believe, 9, 11-12, 25, 41, 45, 52, 65,
    79, 107, 177-178, 189, 196,
    198, 204
Bellows, 55
Beloved, 33, 79, 83, 141
Belt, 58
Bethlehem, 159, 163, 166

About the Author

His name is Hebrew סמאל און ואור, and is pronounced "sam-ayel on vay-or." You may not have heard of him, but Samael Aun Weor changed the world.

In 1950, in his first two books, he became the first person to reveal the esoteric secret hidden in all the world's great religions, and for that, accused of "healing the ill," he was put in prison. Nevertheless, he did not stop. Between 1950 and 1977 — merely twenty-seven years — not only did Samael Aun Weor write over sixty books on the most difficult subjects in the world, such as consciousness, kabbalah, physics, tantra, meditation, etc., in which he deftly exposed the singular root of all knowledge — which he called Gnosis — he simultaneously inspired millions of people across the entire span of Latin America: stretching across twenty countries and an area of more than 21,000,000 square kilometers, founding schools everywhere, even in places without electricity or post offices.

During those twenty-seven years, he experienced all the extremes that humanity could give him, from adoration to death threats, and in spite of the enormous popularity of his books and lectures, he renounced an income, refused recognitions, walked away from accolades, and consistently turned away those who would worship him. He held as friends both presidents and peasants, and yet remained a mystery to all.

When one reflects on the effort and will it requires to perform even day to day tasks, it is astonishing to consider the herculean efforts required to accomplish what he did in such a short time. But, there is a reason: he was a man who knew who he was, and what he had to do. A true example of compassion and selfless service, Samael Aun Weor dedicated the whole of his life to freely helping anyone and everyone find the path out of suffering. His mission was to show all of humanity the universal source of all spiritual traditions, which he did not only through his writings and lectures, but also through his actions. He said,

"I, the one who writes this book, am not anyone's master, and I beg people to not follow me. I am an imperfect human just like anyone else, and it is an error to follow someone who is imperfect. Let every one follow their "I am [their Innermost]...

"I do not want to receive visitors. Unquestionably, I am nothing more than a postman, a courier, a man that delivers a message... It would be the breaking point of silliness for you to come from your country to the capital city of Mexico with the only purpose of visiting a vulgar postman, an employee that delivered you a letter in the past... Why would you waste your money for that? Why would you visit a simple courier, a miserable postman? It is better for you to study the message, the written teachings delivered in the books...

"I have not come to form any sect, or one more belief, nor am I interested in the schools of today, or the particular beliefs of anyone! ...

"We are not interested in anyone's money, nor are we interested in monthly fees, or temples made out of brick, cement or clay, because we are conscious visitors in the cathedral of the soul and we know that wisdom is of the soul.

"Flattery tires us, praise should only belong to our Father (who is in secret and watches over us minutely).

"We are not in search of followers; all we want is for each person to follow his or her self—their own internal master, their sacred Innermost—because he is the only one who can save and glorify us.

"I do not follow anyone, therefore no one should follow me...

"We do not want any more comedies, pretenses, false mysticism, or false schools. What we want now are living realities; we want to prepare ourselves to see, hear, and touch the reality of those truths..."

Your book reviews matter.

Glorian Publishing is a very small non-profit organization, thus we have no money to spend on marketing and advertising. Fortunately, there is a proven way to gain the attention of readers: book reviews. Mainstream book reviewers won't review these books, but you can.

The path of liberation requires the daily balance of three active factors:

- birth of virtue
- death of vice
- sacrifice for others

Writing book reviews is a powerful way to sacrifice for others. By writing book reviews on popular websites, you help to make the books more visible to humanity, and you might help save a soul from suffering. Will you do your part to help us show these wonderful teachings to others? Take a moment today to write a review.

Donate

Glorian Publishing is a non-profit publisher dedicated to spreading the sacred universal doctrine to suffering humanity. All of our works are made possible by the kindness and generosity of sponsors. If you would like to make a tax-deductible donation, you may send it to the address below, or visit our website for other alternatives. If you would like to sponsor the publication of a book, please contact us at (844) 945-6742 or help@glorian.org.

Glorian Publishing
PO Box 209
Clinton, CT 06413 US
Phone: (844) 945-6742
VISIT US ONLINE AT glorian.org